How the West Indian Child
is made educationally *sub*-normal
in the British School System

FIFTIETH ANNIVERSARY
EXPANDED 5TH EDITION

BERNARD COARD

How the West Indian Child is made educationally sub-normal in the British School System, 5th edition

McDermott Publishing
Kingston, Jamaica • St. George's, Grenada
Email: mcdermottpublishing@gmail.com

ISBN: 9798703252703

First Edition 1971 by New Beacon Books, on behalf of CECWA (Caribbean Education and Community Workers' Association)

Second Edition 1991 by Karia Press

Third Edition 2005 & Fourth Edition 2007 co-published by Bookmarks Publications and Trentham Books, in Brian Richardson (Ed.), *Tell It Like It Is: How Our Schools Fail Black Children*

Photos of Author:
Courtesy of Cheryl Coard (back cover) and Clinton Hutton (p.103)

Fifth edition book and cover design by A. Lewinson-Morgan
Set in Iowan Old Style 11/14pt with CgPhenixAmerican and Helvetica

IN MEMORY OF

Phyllis Coard

MY BELOVED WIFE, LIFE PARTNER
& SOULMATE

2nd November 1943 – 6th September 2020

IN MEMORIAM

JOHN LA ROSE

Visionary, Activist, Writer,
Poet, Educator, Publisher

27th December 1927 – 28th February 2006

JESSICA ELLESSIE HUNTLEY

Visionary, Indefatigable Fighter,
Motivator, Publisher

23rd February 1927 – 13th October 2013

NORRIS CHRISLEVENTON "BUZZ" JOHNSON

Activist,
Publisher Extraordinaire

2nd November 1951 – 11th February 2014

This book is dedicated to

My Parents

and

All Black Parents

who value their Children's education
and opportunities in Life above all else.

Contents

Contents

Introduction
to the 5th Edition

by Paul Mackney

Bernard Coard's 1971 booklet remains the most important contribution to anti-racist educational theory and practice for multi-cultural Britain. The issues raised by the 'Black Lives Matter' movement show its continuing relevance.

Coard said he wrote it for the West Indian Community in Britain, but it also jolted teachers into examining how they were teaching, with what expectations and in what sort of institutions. Coard described institutional racism in terms which allocated all the key actors a role either in perpetuating or eliminating the phenomenon.

Rae Davis, former Principal of Jamaica University of Technology, recalled that 'in 1971 we were somewhat on the back foot and losing our confidence, but Coard's pamphlet changed all that'. Hans Eysenck and other 'experts' had been saying that Black people were less intelligent than whites. Coard pinpointed the self-fulfilling fallacy: Black children were failed by the education system because they were not expected to achieve. Coard argued in an additional essay, 'High Quality Education for All', that 'when society fails one generation of children, it lays the foundations for similar, even worse failures in the generations to follow. We human beings "inherit" not only through our genes, but often also from our social circumstances.'

Almost thirty years later, Natfhe (now in the University and College Union) set up a task force to consider the educational implications of the Stephen Lawrence Report which had identified institutional racism in the police. Its first task was to see how far the practices identified in Coard's booklet had been addressed.

Soon we hit a snag: we couldn't buy a copy anywhere. So we ran off 50 copies on the general secretary's photocopier. They soon went. There was a steady trickle of requests for more – particularly from teacher educators.

So, backed by the London Mayor and edited by Brian Richardson, a new edition of Coard's booklet was printed as the lead essay in a compilation of thirty contributions forming *Tell It Like It Is: How Our Schools Fail Black Children*. Two editions soon sold out!

— PAUL MACKNEY
Former General Secretary of UCU (Natfhe)

January 12, 2021

Foreword
to the 5ᵗʰ Edition

by Rt. Hon. Jeremy Corbyn, M.P.

I am delighted that Bernard's 1971 publication of 'How the West Indian Child is Made Educationally Sub-Normal in the British School System' is being once again republished.

It was last republished in 1991 by the excellent Karia Press in Haringey.

I had the honour of meeting Bernard in my Parliamentary office as leader of the Opposition and we talked about his life, his work and his time in prison in Grenada after the US occupation in 1983. I visited Grenada in 1983 after the invasion, and with my friend, the late Bernie Grant, we attempted to visit Bernard and the other detainees in prison. We were denied that opportunity but later met Sir Paul Scoon, the Governor General, and argued their case very strongly. The death penalty was a very real threat.

Later, during his long imprisonment, Bernard effectively became, with others, the prison's Education System and taught and inspired many prisoners to make the best of their lives. Bernard was, is and always will be, an educator.

The context of the booklet was the racism of 1960s' Britain, exemplified by Enoch Powell and notions of racial superiority, and the treatment of the Black community, and of course their children.

Bernard's booklet was written from his life experience as a teacher and the way in which Black children from the Caribbean were underachieving in school and that a wholly disproportionate number were declared to be 'educationally subnormal' and placed in schools so named. Indeed in 1967, 28.4 per cent of the ESN school roll in the ILEA was of children from Caribbean families, even though they formed only 15 per cent of the mainstream school population.

Bernard explored the reasons for this and found a combination of racist attitudes by some teachers, the white middle-class attitudes of schools and the biased testing methods of all schools, in particular the 11+ examination.

Bernard and Phyllis had a big influence in the Caribbean community in Haringey and that in turn forced the Labour Party in that Borough to pledge an end to the 'banding system' in its schools in the 1971 Council elections. I remember arguing this case on the doorsteps in that election and was three years later a Councillor arguing the case not just for ending banding but also for a change in history teaching and the opening of a Caribbean Community Centre.

Amongst the recommendations in the booklet were the support and promotion of community organisations. The purpose of the booklet was to empower the community and give practical support and advice to parents who were nervous of approaching their children's schools.

For me it is an enormous pleasure to know that New Beacon Bookshop, opened by John LaRose and the community is still there, supplying me with books I need and giving the African-Caribbean community a place to explore history and attitudes.

In republication of this work, we see how important the message that Bernard gave was, and how we must take it further forward.

Racism is vile, racist attitudes are vile and waste lives. How many children forced into ESN schools in the 1960s were unable to reach their potential, giving them less fulfilling lives, and for the community as a whole denied the benefit of their potential skills and contribution to our lives.

Racism does not rise in a vacuum.

The teaching of history to our children has a huge impact on attitudes. Our children need to understand global history and the contribution to learning and invention by peoples from all over the world. The notion of racial superiority enabled the slave trade and colonisation to take place.

'Black Lives Matter' is a product of the brutality of the US police force towards the Black community and has had a dramatic effect worldwide. Marginalised, discriminated against and oppressed people the world over saw something of their experience in the killing of George Floyd.

Republication is welcome as it gives another impetus to promote a real understanding of history and the joy of global literature and understanding.

— RT. HON. JEREMY CORBYN, M.P.

Former Leader of the Opposition
in the British Parliament

January 11, 2021

Notes ...

Preface

to the 5th Edition

» Weapons of Mass Suppression

Back in 1971 when this booklet was first published, the principal Weapons of Mass Suppression, or WMS, of Black Caribbean children's educational and life prospects were the ESN school, ESN streams and 'Remedial' classes in regular schools. New versions of WMS appeared over the ensuing decades, as the original model, and each replacement, met with Black Caribbean resistance and even open protest. Schools for 'Children With Learning Difficulties', schools for the 'Emotionally and Behaviourly Disturbed' (EBD), and 'Pupil Referral Units' (PRUs) took their turns in the arsenal of Black educational suppression.

In each case, the objective of these 'new' iterations was not to concentrate more resources and more experienced and skilled teachers to meet the needs of the children designated as 'in Special Educational Need (SEN)', but rather to assign less of these resources, and less experienced teachers to their care. It was a dustbin solution, not a lifting-the-child-up operation. It was a life sentence, not a life-line to greater opportunities.

Additional devices for suppression also emerged. Although the scale of 'Exclusions' of Black Caribbean children reached alarming proportions in the 1980s, '90s and beyond, this suppression device had shown its head as early as the '70s to such an extent that Black Caribbean parents' complaints about it are referred to in the 1981 Rampton Report.[1]

---

1   A. Rampton, 'West Indian Children in Our Schools' (1981).

Gillborn and Youdell[2] and several other scholars would expose the use of 'Setting' and 'Tiering' to suppress the academic prospects of Black Caribbean children. These were essentially devices to prevent these children from being permitted to sit exams at a level which would open up prospects for further education and thus for higher employment opportunities. Their research revealed that preventing Black Caribbean children from sitting examinations at certain levels was done with zero input from the students or parents involved, or even knowledge that this was being done – echoes of the ESN schools model of keeping parents in the dark while taking measures to destroy their children's educational and life prospects.

Viewed from the perspective of the extraordinary array of educational WMS unleashed on Black Caribbean children over the past half-century and more, it is remarkable that the academic performance gap between Black Caribbean children (taken as a whole) and White British children is not far greater than it is. Indeed, Professor Devonish draws attention in Part 3 of this expanded 50th Anniversary Edition to official statistics suggesting that Black Caribbean boys eligible for free school meals outperform White British boys eligible for school meals, and Black Caribbean girls outperform White British girls in similar socio-economic circumstances by an even greater percentage. Professor Devonish cautiously observes that:

> 'There is a pattern here, that at the lowest income level, gender for gender, the Black Caribbean ethnic group seems to be outperforming its White British counterpart.'

2　David Gillborn and Deborah Youdell, *Rationing Education: Policy, Practice, Reform and Equity* (2000). See also David Gillborn, 'Education policy as an act of white supremacy: Whiteness, critical race theory and education reform'. *Journal of Education Policy, Vol. 20*, No. 4 (July 2005).

Preface

❱ 'Social Capital' and Black Caribbean Resistance

What, then, has made it possible for many Black Caribbean children, despite still performing well below their potential, to do as well as they have in the face of sustained educational WMS thrown at them throughout their schooling? The key has been the Social Capital of the Caribbean community in Britain. It is also the key going forward, to taking the struggle to a higher and more successful level, but this will be explored more fully in the near future.

Social Capital is the 'glue' which holds people together, encourages collective action in solving problems; motivates individuals and families to help other individuals and families in need without expectation of personal reward. Social Capital is formed out of a common sense of identity, shared values and expectations, and a willingness to come together to tackle major problems and especially crises. In turn, acting together helps to build more Social Capital.

Most Caribbean immigrants of the late 1940s, the '50s and '60s – the 'Windrush generation' – came, at that time, with minimal academic or professional certification, and little or no knowledge that their children were being systematically denied even a half-decent education. However, what the vast majority of these parents shared in common was a burning desire for their children to succeed at school and hence later in life.

Once the realization dawned that their pride and joy, their children, were being systematically held down, the community became galvanized. As I narrate in Part 2 of this edition, the original 1971 edition of this book arose out of a series of collective actions by Caribbean community leaders. It would never have been written without them. The mushrooming of Black Caribbean parents groups, and the explosion in Black Caribbean Supplementary Schools, were all a product and expression of Black Caribbean Social Capital.

❱ Future Progress Depends on Strengthening Social Capital, and Building Alliances...

Most folks understand the importance of Physical Capital (land, housing, factories, stores, and so on), Financial Capital (funds in the banks, stocks and shares, financial investments of all sorts) and Human Capital (individual academic, professional, para-professional, individual skill-sets of all kinds). Few, however, appreciate the enormous importance of Social Capital to the success of so many immigrant ethnic groups in so many countries including Britain; nor what happens when Social Capital becomes eroded (whether by drugs, alcohol, a gradual loss of identity and shared values, loss of cohesion through the development of violent feuds within the community, and so on). I happen to believe that, of all the forms of Capital, Social Capital is the most important; indeed, it can be used to create and expand the other forms of Capital.[3]

Professor Devonish notes in his contribution in Part 3 the performance of the many other ethnic groups in Britain. Significantly, most if not all of these immigrant ethnic groups have started their own versions of Supplementary education for their children. Their rising success, I believe, is a product of their more highly developed and deployed Social Capital. We Caribbean folks can learn from them, to strengthen and diversify our forms of Supplementary education for our children.

In the second half of Part 2 of this 5th Edition, I explore not only how decisive quality education is for all Black Caribbean children in Britain, but how critical it is for Caribbean communities throughout Britain to strike alliances with other groups around the rallying cry of 'Quality Education For All!'. Despite

---

3   On a relatively small scale, this is what the 'su-su' or 'pardoner' practices of Caribbean people involve: using Trust, and Collective Action – that is, Social Capital – to get a small business established or expanded; thus leveraging Social Capital to build Physical and/or Financial Capital. We are aware that other immigrant ethnic groups have done this on a far larger and more diversified scale than we Caribbean folks. We should learn from them!

the ravages of the WMS thrown at our children for over half a century, close to 40 per cent, or 4 in every 10 have been able to make some headway even while not achieving as much as they could have in a less racist system. Our goal, however, is not only to take that 40 per cent further up the ladder of educational – and job – attainment, but to also elevate the remaining 6 in 10 still mired, still crushed, in the present system.

The key, I believe, is to greatly strengthen and effectively deploy our Caribbean Social Capital to raise to a higher level our Caribbean communities' enhancement of ALL our children's education, including further positive self-image and self-belief work; in the process close down the conveyor belt from school exclusions to prison; and more energetically strike alliances with groups and organizations of all kinds to achieve these and related objectives.

The last 50 years has taught us not to rely on pleas to or the goodwill of those running the system to effect the changes our children need. Just as we did a half-century ago and since, we have to accept that future progress for our children on all fronts depends on our actions, our initiatives, our building up and energetically deploying our Social Capital, and our striking alliances with all those who are prepared to join us in this struggle to achieve quality education for all!

—B.C.

January 26, 2021

Acknowledgments

I am indebted to John La Rose and Jessica Huntley for the inspiration and encouragement for writing this book; to Winston Best to Waveney Bushell and Van Rigsby for their criticism and advice; to my wife Phyllis, without whose constant advice, moral support and typing skill this book would have been impossible.

Finally I am indebted to the many people and the West Indian organizations who have contributed to the publication and distribution of this book.

—B.C.

❯ Acknowledgements to the 5th Edition

In addition to all those acknowledged in the first and second editions, as also those acknowledged in the 'Tell It Like It Is' editions of 2005 and 2007, along with the many distinguished contributors to those editions, the author wishes to place on record his deep gratitude to the following persons who have contributed in so many ways:

Minka Adofoh	Tim Brighouse
Kehinde Andrews	Abiola Coard
Jane Atkins	Sola Coard
Constance Bartholomew	Jeremy Corbyn
Dennis Bartholomew	Polly Curtis
Robert Beckford	Steve Cushion
Roy Bedeau	Luke Daniels
Akhita Benjamin	Hubert Devonish
Cauline Braithwaite	Kelvin Edmond

Acknowledgments

Funmi
Shey Fyffe
Rob 'Bussa' Graham
Ruth Hayes
Anne Hickling-Hudson
Brian Hudson
Eric Huntley
John 'Rocky' Joseph
Tumaini Joseph
Paddy Kerwin
Jenna Khalfan
Afshan Khan
Annika Lewinson-Morgan
Andre Lewis
Ida Lewis
Paul Mackney
Liam Martin
Jacqui McKenzie
Kate Quinn
Omowale Ru Pert-em-hru

Brian Richardson
Jane Ritchie
Alan Scott
Noreen Scott
Chris Searle
Ludi Simpson
Richard Skyers
Edward 'Ed' David Spring
Crofton St Louis
Maureen Stone
Peter Stone
Selwyn Strachan
Bob Stoker
Jean Tate
Ewart Thomas
Sally Tomlinson
Judy Tregenza
Verna Wilkins
Derek Wilson

Abbreviations

CSE	Certificate of Secondary Education (exam)
EBD	Emotionally and Behaviourly Disturbed
ESN	educationally subnormal
FSM	free school meals
GCSE	General Certificate of Secondary Education
ILEA	Inner London Education Authority
IQ	intelligence quotient
MSN	mentally subnormal
'O' Levels	General Certificate of Education (GCE) Ordinary Level exam
PE	Physical Education
PISA	Programme for International Student Assessment
PRU	Pupil Referral Unit
SEN	Special Educational Needs
SSN	severely subnormal
Three Rs	reading, writing and (a)rithmetic
UK	United Kingdom
US	United States
USA	United States of America
WMS	Weapons of Mass Suppression

PART 1

How the West Indian Child
Is Made Educationally Sub-Normal
in the British School System

Notes...

CHAPTER 1

West Indian Children in ESN (Special) Schools in Britain

There are five main points I want to bring to the attention of West Indian parents and others interested:

1 • There are very large numbers of our West Indian children in schools for the Educationally Sub-Normal – which is what ESN means.

2 • These children have been wrongly placed there.

3 • Once placed in these schools, the vast majority never get out and return to normal schools.

4 • They suffer academically and in their job prospects for life because of being put in these schools.

5 • The authorities are doing *very* little to stop this scandal.

❱ Large Numbers

An Inner London Education Authority (ILEA) report entitled *The Education of Immigrant Pupils in Special Schools for Educationally Subnormal Children* (ILEA 657) reveals that five of their secondary ESN schools had more than 30 per cent immigrant pupils at the time of their survey in 1967. By January 1968, one of the schools had 60 per cent immigrant children!

In the ILEA's ESN (Special) Day Schools, over 28 per cent of all the pupils are immigrant, compared with only 15 per cent immigrants in the ordinary schools of the ILEA. This situation is particularly bad for the West Indians, because three-quarters of all the immigrant children in these Educationally Subnormal schools are West Indian, whereas West Indians are only half of the immigrant population in the ordinary schools. The 1970 figures are even more alarming, for even though immigrants comprised nearly 17 per cent of the normal school population nearly 34 percent of the ESN school population is immigrant. And four out of every five immigrant children in these ESN schools are West Indian. The figures from the ILEA report to substantiate what I have said above are given at the back of this booklet in Appendix I.

❯ Wrongful Placement

The same ILEA report gives figures of immigrant children whom the headmasters of these ESN schools thought were wrongly assessed and placed:

Three of the nineteen schools thought that less than 10 per cent of their immigrant pupils had been wrongly placed; three thought that between 10 and 19 per cent were wrongly placed; a further three thought that the figure was between 20 and 29 per cent. One school put the figure at between 30 and 39 per cent; two schools thought as many as 40 to 49 per cent of the immigrant pupils were wrongly placed; and finally, one school estimated that between 70 and 79 per cent of its immigrant pupils were wrongly placed!

Thus nine out of nineteen schools thought that 20 per cent or more of their immigrant pupils had been wrongly placed. This is from Table 9, page 9, of the ILEA report. The report states on page 5 that: 'Where children are suspected as being wrongly placed in the ESN school, this is *four times as likely* in the case of immigrant pupils' (my italics).

❯ Permanently ESN

On the question of the number of children returning to normal schools, the report states (page 3): 'The number returning to ordinary schools ... is low, and is only slightly higher for immigrants (7 per cent) than for non-immigrants (4 per cent).' From this we can see clearly that even though massive numbers of West Indian and other immigrant children are being wrongly placed in these ESN schools, only 7 *per cent* ever return to normal schools. We must therefore arrive at the conclusion that the West Indian child's frequently wrongful placement in an ESN school is a one-way educational ticket.

❯ Why the ESN School is Unsuitable for the Child Who Has Been Wrongly Placed

In order to understand why it is so scandalous for large numbers of West Indian children to be wrongly placed in ESN schools – and never get the opportunity to return to normal schools – one must understand the nature of the ESN school, how it is organised, and who it caters for.

ESN schools are designed to assist each child in such a school to realise his *assumed low* capabilities so that he will on leaving school be able to hold down a simple job and be as independent as possible, thereby not being a burden on his family or the State when in adult life. The whole assumption of an ESN school is that the child cannot cope with the average academic requirements of a normal school.

The children are chosen to attend these schools because they are of low intelligence: 50 to 75 or 80 IQ. Children of normal intelligence are supposed to score between 90 and 110 on the IQ tests. The Education Act of 1921 defined ESN children as those who 'not being imbecile' and not being merely 'dull and backward' should be provided for in special classes and schools. Therefore, if a child were an 'imbecile' (in other words, of under 50 IQ), nowadays referred to as 'severely subnormal' (SSN), he would be placed in a hospital or training centre. If he were 'merely dull and backward', then he would still remain in an ordinary school, with perhaps extra help. To be ESN under the 1921 Act, you need to be *very* dull or backward, but not so much as to be an 'imbecile'.

Under the 1944 Education Act, local education authorities were directed 'to the need for securing that provision is made for pupils who suffer from any disability of mind or body by providing, either in special schools or otherwise, special educational treatment, that is to say, education by special methods appropriate for persons suffering from that disability'. It was intended that Special Schools would provide mainly for pupils whose backwardness was due to *limited ability*. Pupils who were not so limited intellectually would need suitable arrangements in ordinary school.[4]

I have run youth clubs for children from seven ESN schools in London. I have visited these schools on several occasions, as well as others. I have taught in two ESN schools over the past two years. I have held numerous conversations and discussion with the head teachers and staff of these many schools. The main purpose of an ESN school which emerges from my experience and observation, is to 'socialise' the child, rather than attempt academic wonders with him. The child must be provided with a structure which facilitates his learning to live with himself and with other children, and with adults. This seems to be priority number one. If he is to cope with society given his low intelligence, initial sense of failure, and his general

---

4 For evidence of this, see A.E. Tansley and R. Gulliford, *The Education of Slow-learning Children* (1960); especially pages 1-22.

lack of confidence, he must be taught, through the provision of the right environment, how to cope with his own emotional problems and how to relate or 'get on' with the other children.

This task quite often takes up the best part of the child's years at the ESN school, and so most children hardly get beyond this stage to the stage where they can grasp the 'three Rs' in other than a rudimentary way. Given their low intellectual capacity, this is undoubtedly the right emphasis in their education (always assuming, of course, that the children's intelligence has been correctly assessed, which it has not in the case of most West Indian children). The true ESN child can never expect realistically to be given the sort of job which calls for academic qualifications or an average level of intellectual reasoning. Given his limited mental ability, he is placed in a job which is simple, repetitive, requires little initiative, and a minimum of mental effort. Such a job he can manage. A job requiring greater mental skills he would probably fail at, with grave repercussions for his mental health. Once he is given sufficient instruction in the three Rs so that he can cope with signs, notices, simple correspondence, and basic arithmetic, the most important qualification he must possess if he is to hold down a job in society, is that of *social adjustment*, namely, being able to get on with the boss and fellow workers and not lose job after job.

Naturally, each school tries to do more than the rudimentary three Rs with children who are capable of more wherever and whenever possible. Some children leave school with the ability to read some books. However, the extent to which this can be done is limited by the fact that the teachers have to concentrate on basic arithmetic, reading and writing, along with woodwork, needlework, cookery, swimming, PE, etcetera, and cannot teach the whole range of subjects like geography, history, biology, English literature, physics, etcetera, which would broaden considerably the horizons of the averagely intelligent child. It would be quite impractical to teach all the subjects at an

ESN school given the staff size, school library facilities and the intellectual calibre of the pupils who have been specially placed there. It would also be educationally wrong, since, as explained earlier, the major need of the children is for social adequacy. It is only because ESN schools build up a special library of books to deal with the children's basic reading difficulties, arrange a curriculum which helps these children of low ability, and choose the right staff for the job, that they are at all able to help the educationally subnormal child and prepare him for his role in society. If they were to perform the same duties as a normal school, or do both jobs, they would be unable to do either properly.

Therefore, ESN schools are not places where children go for short periods of six months to two years in order to be given intensive and highly specialised help so that they can then be returned to normal schools and function at the normal academic level. Many West Indian parents in my experience have been led to believe that they are, and have therefore been quite happy to let their children attend these 'Special' schools, believing them to be especially good. This explains why many have not protested at their child's assignment to one of these schools. Another reason is that many are never told that they have the right of appeal over the assessment.

If the ESN school did prepare the child through intensive lessons for coping in the ordinary school, then West Indian children by and large would perhaps be rightly placed. Instead because children are attached to these schools on a *permanent basis,* the curriculum and entire organisation of the school is geared to cope with children who are of below normal academic abilities. It is true that the range of ability in an ESN school is very large, since it copes with 50 to 80 IQ levels. But though the range is large, it is, as a whole, well below average academic standards. The children are being prepared for *survival,* not for *excelling,* or even participating actively in the society as does the average person.

From what I have said so far, it is quite clear that the academic organisation of the ESN school is not geared for coping (and quite rightly) with a child of average or above average intelligence. A Black child of average or above average intelligence who gets placed in an ESN school can be expected to encounter great difficulties. The child who feels he is wrongly placed (and many do feel this way) may become upset or even disturbed and refuse to cooperate or participate fully in the classroom, and so will appear even more retarded – and become retarded through mental inactivity – as time goes by.

The experience of being removed from a normal school and placed in the neighbourhood 'nut' school, as everyone calls it, is a bitter one. The child feels deeply that racial discrimination and rejection have been practised towards him by the authorities who assessed him wrongly as being ESN. Other Black children, who are young and unsure of themselves, may simply accept the judgement of themselves as being of low intelligence and give up any attempt to succeed academically. The immense influence of other people's expectations in creating the child's own self-image of his abilities and likely performance will be examined, with evidence, in Chapter 3.

On the other side of the coin, the teacher who is told by the educational 'experts' that a child is ESN, will obviously *expect* the child to *be* ESN. Therefore, the sort of work she will give the child, and the standard she will expect of him, will obviously be much lower than in a normal school. This means the child will learn much less than he is really capable of, and will be very frustrated day by day in the class room. That such children quite often 'act up' and become behaviour problems under these circumstances is to be expected.

However, even if:

(1) the teacher had the full range of books and teaching equipment which an ordinary school has, and

(2) had the right expectations of the child's intellectual ability, and

(3) the West Indian child were not in the least bit affected by being taken out of ordinary school and placed in a school with educationally subnormal and in many cases emotionally disturbed children,

– all highly unlikely assumptions – the problem of keeping one or two children of average intelligence not only just 'occupied' but educationally stimulated, and advancing at a normal academic rate, while at the same time trying to teach eighteen or nineteen other children at a considerably different academic (and emotional) level, would be virtually impossible.

The implications for the large number of West Indian children who get placed in ESN schools and who can never 'escape' back to normal schools are far reaching and permanent. As demonstrated above, the West Indian child's educational level on leaving school will be very low. He will be eligible, by reason of his lack of qualifications and his assessment as being ESN, only for the jobs which *really*-ESN pupils are able to perform; namely, simple, repetitive jobs of a menial kind, which involve little use of intelligence. This is what he or she can look forward to as a career! In turn, through his getting poor wages, poor housing, and having no motivation to better himself, his children can look forward to a similar educational experience and similar career prospects! No wonder E.J.B. Rose, who was Director of the Survey of Race Relations in Britain, and co-author of the report *Colour and Citizenship,* states that by the year 2000 Britain will probably have a Black helot class unless the educational system is radically altered.[5]

As Maureen Stone points out in her thesis, *West Indian children in an ESN school – why are they there?*: 'The Authorities should realise that by placing these children in ESN schools

---

5 *The Times*, 15 May 1970, page 11. A *helot* is a modern-day 'hewer of wood and drawer of water'.

they are not solving a problem, but creating one, for these same children will grow up to react with hatred and violence against a system that has crippled them by making them in one other respect (education) unable to play their full role in society.'

▶ The Authorities Do Nothing

One can appreciate from the evidence presented just how imperative and urgent it is to *stop and reverse* the process by which these large numbers of immigrant and especially West Indian children are being dumped in ESN schools. One would have thought that in the light of their own report on this scandal, the ILEA inspectorate would have recommended the reversal of present policy. Instead, the ILEA report (657) states in its first recommendation (page 6): 'Special Schools for ESN children must continue to provide for immigrant children, *even those of relatively high IQ,* until more suitable alternative provision can be made. The recommendation must always be based on the educational needs of the child'! (my italics).

The entire report reeks of complacency, and no urgent recommendations are made at all. The ILEA and other local education authorities in Britain have continued to treat the problem with the same complacency, and the numbers of West Indian children admitted to ESN schools continue to soar. But then, perhaps it is not complacency on the part of the authorities, but rather a conscious plan. Perhaps. The evidence for this argument will be presented in Chapter 7.

CHAPTER 2

Why Are Our Children Wrongly Placed?

❱ Personal Biases in Assessment

There are numerous reasons for such large numbers of West Indian children being wrongly placed in ESN special schools. They revolve around the *manner of assessment* by the authorities. In many authorities, only the Medical Officer of Health decides, which is farcical, since he has no qualifications in this field. In other authorities, a committee including the headmaster of the child's school and the Educational Psychologist decides. Usually the opinion of the Educational Psychologist is decisive. In turn, the single most important indicator to the Educational Psychologist is the *IQ test*.

Immediately, two problems arise from this. The Teacher in the classroom, whose report initiates the assessment proceedings, the Headmaster, and the Educational Psychologist impose three biases quite often in their assessment of the child.

> ❭ *The Cultural Bias:* This normally takes the form of linguistic difference between West Indian English and 'standard classroom' English. The West Indian child's choice of words, usage and meaning of words, pronunciation, and intonation sometimes present tremendous difficulties in communication with the teacher, *and vice versa*. This factor, while recognised in a lip service way by many of the teachers and other authorities involved, is often ignored when assessing and generally relating with the child. Thus, teachers often presume to describe West Indian children

as being 'dull', when in fact no educated assessment of the child's intelligence can be made under these circumstances. In addition, many behaviour patterns and ways of relating to the teacher and to other children which are part of the West Indian culture are misunderstood by the teacher, who usually has no understanding of or inclination to learn about the West Indian culture. The ILEA report (page 10) points out that only three of the nineteen schools suggested as a helpful method the training of teachers about the culture of the immigrant's country. While certain initial attempts are being made to educate teachers in this direction, the scope and direction of the programme – and the people running it – make one very sceptical about its usefulness.

One common difficulty, for instance, arises from the fact that the child is not expected to talk and 'talk back' as much in the West Indian classroom as he is here, in the English classroom. English teachers tend to interpret this apparent shyness and relative unresponsiveness as indicating either silent hostility or low intelligence. Many teachers have said to me that only after years of experience have they discovered that often when the West Indian child does not understand what they are saying, he replies 'Yes', because he thinks this is expected of him in his relationship to the teacher. Moreover, many children fear that they may arouse the teacher's anger or be thought stupid if they ask her to repeat what she has said.

> *The Middle Class Bias:* In most cases, the teacher and the Educational Psychologist are middle class, in a middle-class institution (which is what a school is), viewing the child through middle-class tinted glasses, the child being working class in most cases. Both on the basis of class and culture, they believe their standards to be the right and superior ones. They may do this in the most casual and unconscious of ways, which may make the effect on the child even more devastating. The child may, therefore, not

13

only because of problems with language but also because of feeling that he is somehow inferior, and bound to fail, refuse to communicate or to try his best in the tests for assessment. Evidence to support this statement will be given in Chapters 3 and 4.

> *The Emotional Disturbance Bias:* Many of the problem children, I would contend, are suffering a temporary emotional disturbance due to severe culture and family shock, resulting from their sudden removal from the West Indies to a half-forgotten family, and an unknown and generally hostile environment. They often react by being withdrawn and uncommunicative, or, alternatively, by acting out aggressively, both of which are well-known human reactions to upset, bewilderment and dislocation. This behaviour is often misunderstood by these supposedly trained people, as being a permanent disturbance. Despite their training, in my experience, many teachers feel threatened by disturbed children and tend to be biased against them. This accounts for the extremely large numbers of West Indian children who are submitted for assessment by the teachers not on grounds of intellectual capacity, but because they are 'a bloody nuisance'. And dozens of teachers and head teachers have admitted this to me.

This temporary disturbance of the children due to the emotional shocks they have suffered may well take on a permanent form, however, when the nature of their problem and their consequent needs are misunderstood, and instead they face an educational environment which is humiliating and rejecting.[6] While suffering emotional turmoil they are placed in unfamiliar testing situations, to do unfamiliar and culturally biased tests, with white examiners whose speech is different, whom they have been brought up to identify as

---

6   See Chapters 3 and 5.

the 'master class',[7] and before whom they expect to fail. They then experience the test, only to have their fears confirmed, when they are removed from normal schools – in their mind, 'rejected' – and placed in the neighbourhood 'nut' school. And it must be remembered that the ILEA report states (page 3) that 20 per cent (that is, one-fifth) of all the immigrant pupils in six of their secondary ESN schools had been admitted to the Special School without even being given a trial in ordinary school first.

» The IQ Test

All three biases against the West Indian child, cultural, middle class, and emotional disturbance, apply just as much to the actual questions asked on the IQ test administered to the children, and the very nature of 'the test situation'. The vocabulary and style of all these IQ tests is white middle class. Many of the questions are capable of being answered by a white middle-class boy, who, because of being middle class, has the right background of experiences with which to answer the questions – regardless of his real intelligence. The Black working-class child, who has different life experiences, finds great difficulty in answering many of the questions, even if he is very intelligent.

The very fact of being 'tested' is a foreign experience to many Black children. The white middle-class child is used to tests. The questions that are asked on these tests have to do with the sort of life he lives. He is therefore confident when doing these tests. Thus the white middle-class child can be expected to do these tests better than the white working-class or Black child – and he does. If white middle-class people make up these IQ tests, and if they also do the testing, is it really any surprise that their own children score the highest? Does this have anything to do with the real abilities of the children? None.

7 See Chapter 4.

Similarly, it should be pointed out that an emotionally disturbed child is highly likely to do badly in tests, since the act of sitting in one place for an hour or more, and answering a series of questions and doing a series of different tasks in a special order, is likely to be too frustrating and confining an experience for him.

IQ tests can only be claimed to measure intellectual functioning *at a particular moment in time, without being able to give the reasons why the functioning is at that particular level, or say which factors are more important than which for each child tested.* This point is vital to grasp if one is to understand why the IQ test is meaningless in so many cases.

The child may be functioning below normal because of being emotionally disturbed, or because of being in a bad mood on the day of the test. It could be because of racial resentment at being tested by a white person (see Chapter 4), or the fear of being placed in an ESN school as a result of the test. It could be the result of low motivation to do or succeed on the test; or it could be the fact that the act of being tested is a foreign or unusual experience, and hence the child is nervous and possibly even upset. Any or all of these factors is enough to upset his true score by as much as twenty or more points! And all of this is assuming that the questions on the test itself are not culturally biased – which they are!

Now some of the less honest Educational Psychologists will say that they take account of these factors by stating in their report on the test that the child seemed upset, or disturbed, etcetera. But this does not 'take account' of these vital factors. *There is no assessment or scoring procedure on the IQ test that can add on points to a child's score to take into account any of the disturbance factors. What is most disturbing about the use of the IQ test is that it is the children with difficulties who are on the whole tested.* Therefore, the test is being used in an area where the factors discussed above would most distort the test results; in fact, make it a mockery of an exercise.

Since 20 to 25 points can in many cases decide a child's future, and the test result is very often wrong by a wider margin when dealing with 'problem children', the test is not only a shambles but a tragedy for many.

CHAPTER 3

The Attitude of the Teacher

From what has been said already, it is quite clear that large numbers of West Indian children are failing to perform to the best of their abilities, or even averagely. They are falling behind in their classroom work, and they get low scores on tests, relative to their true abilities. There are many reasons for this, and it is important to know what they are if we are to do anything to alter the situation.

❱ Prejudice and Patronisation

There are three main ways in which a teacher can seriously affect the performance of a Black child: by being openly prejudiced; by being patronising; and by having low expectations of the child's abilities. All three attitudes can be found among teachers in this country. Indeed, these attitudes are widespread. Their effect on the Black child is enormous and devastating.

That there are many openly prejudiced teachers in Britain is not in doubt in my mind. I have experienced them personally. I also have consulted many Black teachers whose experiences with some white teachers are horrifying. Two West Indian teachers in South London have reported to me the cases of white teachers who sit smoking in the staff-room, and refuse to teach a class of nearly-all-Black children. When on one occasion they were accosted by one of the Black teachers, they stated their refusal to teach 'those niggers'. These incidents were reported to the head teachers of the schools, who took no action against the teachers concerned. In fact, the heads of these schools had been trying to persuade the children to leave the school when they had reached school-leaving age, even though their parents wished them to continue their education, in some cases in order to obtain CSEs and 'O' Levels, and in other cases because they thought the children could benefit from another year's general education. Therefore, the teachers in this case conspired to prevent these Black children from furthering their education by simply refusing to teach them.[8]

There are many more teachers who are patronising or condescending towards Black children. These are the sort who treat a Black child as a favourite pet animal. I have often overheard teachers saying: 'I really like that coloured child. He is quite bright for a coloured child!' One teacher actually said to me one day, in a sincere and well-meaning type of voice: 'Gary is really quite a nice boy considering he is Black.' There are other teachers who will not press the Black child too hard academically, as 'he isn't really up to it, poor chap'. Children see through these hypocritical and degrading statements and attitudes more often than adults realise, and they feel deeply aggrieved when anyone treats them as being inferior, which is what patronisation is all about. They build up resentment, and develop emotional blocks to learning.[9]

8 For those who need further detailed evidence of open prejudice by teachers, read Marina Maxwell's 'Violence in the toilets: Experiences of a Black teacher in Brent schools'. *Race Today, Vol. 1* (1969).

9 For further evidence on this and other aspects of the problem, see R.J. Goldman and F.M. Taylor, 'Coloured immigrant children: A survey of research, studies and literature on their educational problems and potential in Britain'. *Educational Research, Vol. 8,* No. 3 (1966).

❱ When the Teacher Does Not Expect Much From the Child

Most teachers absorb the brainwashing that everybody else in the society has absorbed – that Black people are inferior, are less intelligent, etcetera, than white people. Therefore the Black child is expected to do less well in school. The IQ tests which are given to the Black child, with all their cultural bias,[10] give him a low score only too often. The teachers judge the likely ability of the child on the basis of this IQ test. The teacher has, in the form of the IQ test results, what she considers to be 'objective' confirmation of what everybody in the society is thinking and sometimes saying: that the Black children on average have lower IQ than the white children, and must consequently be expected to do less well in class. Alderman Doulton of the Education Committee in the Borough of Haringey has expressed this view, and it is probably fair to say that the banding of children in Haringey for supposedly achieving equal groups of ability in all the schools was really a clever plot to disperse the Black children in the borough throughout the school system. The notorious Professor Jensen, the Enoch Powell of the academic world, has added credence to the myth of Black inferiority by openly declaring that Black people are inherently less intelligent than whites, and therefore Black children should be taught separately.[11]

In these circumstances, it is not surprising that most English teachers expect less from the Black child than from the white child. The profound effect that low teacher expectations has on the child's actual performance will now be illustrated from an experiment conducted in America.

10 See Chapter 2.

11 See Professor Liam Hudson's excellent article on 'IQ: the effect of heredity and environment' in *The Times Saturday Review* (November 7, 1970).

Two American experts in education[12] conducted IQ tests on the children in a particular school in San Francisco. They did not tell the teachers the true results of the tests. Instead, they picked at random twenty names of children from the school and told the teachers that these were the bright children, even though they were not. At the end of the year, the children were tested again, and the teachers were asked many questions about them. The twenty who the teachers *thought* were the brightest did far better than the rest. They got higher scores than the other children in the IQ test. The teachers thought that they were 'happier', more 'curious' and 'interesting' than the other children, and 'more likely to succeed in life than the others'. In Grade 1, the children whom the teachers *thought* were bright gained 27.5 points (on average) in their IQ scores, compared with an average of 12 points for the others, a difference of 15.5 points! In Grade 2, the difference was 9 points.

These scores can make all the difference between whether a child gets into grammar school or not; or which stream a child gets put into in a comprehensive; or whether, indeed, a child will be taken out of an ordinary school and placed in an ESN school. And these performances on the part of the children were simply the result of what the *teachers expected* from each child. They had nothing to do with any special help being given to one group, and the teachers and children were told nothing about the experiment. As the experts pointed out: 'In our experiment, nothing was done directly for the child. There was no crash programme to improve his reading ability, no extra time for tutoring, no programme of trips to museums and art galleries. The only people affected directly were the teachers; the effect on the children was indirect.' Yet they got these large differences in performance directly related to what the teacher expected of the child. This shows how important it is to get rid of these biased IQ tests, conducted under biased conditions; for

12 Robert Rosenthal and L.F. Jacobson, 'Teacher expectations for the disad-vantaged', *Scientific American, Vol. 218*, No. 4 (1968).

the teacher believes in these tests, and the teacher's expectations affect the child's academic progress.

In a study done in London,[13] epileptic children were given an IQ test. Their teachers, not knowing the result of the test, were then asked to give their assessment of the children's intelligence by stating whether a child was 'average', 'above average', 'well above average', etcetera, from their knowledge of each child. It is important to mention at this stage that epileptic children suffer a lot of prejudice directed against them by the general society, similar to that Black children face – but obviously not as great. Teachers also tend to think of them as being less intelligent than ordinary children – again similar to what the Black child faces.

In 28 cases, the teachers seriously underestimated the child's true ability. This means that a *quarter* of the children were wrongly assessed! In one case, a thirteen-year-old girl with an IQ of 120 (which is university level!) had failed her 11+ examination and was in the 'D' stream of a secondary modern school. Her teacher considered that she was of 'below average' intelligence! (Average intelligence = 100.) Another child with family problems and very low income got an IQ score of 132 (which is exceedingly high). Her teachers, however, all rated her as 'low-stream' material!

This sort of information is shocking, because now that most schools are either comprehensive or going comprehensive, it is the assessment of the teachers and head teachers which decides which stream a child is placed in – which in turn influences what is expected of him academically. If these teachers who are supposed to know the children make serious mistakes in a *quarter* of the cases concerning epileptic children, against whom there is *some* prejudice, can you imagine how many wrong assessments are made by teachers when Black children are involved?

13 See C. Bagley, 'The educational performance of immigrant children'. *Race, Vol. 10*, No 1 (1968).

CHAPTER 4

The Black Child's Attitude: Anxiety and Hostility

Studies have been done in America and Britain which show that Black children do considerably worse in tests and exams when they are conducted by white examiners and white Educational Psychologists. In America, Professor Katz proved this beyond all doubt in a series of tests which he conducted with Black children. Whenever a white examiner conducted a test on a Black Child, the Black child always did much worse than when a Black examiner had conducted the test. Whenever the child believed that it was not a test at all, but a game, he always did much better. But the moment the child suspected or was told that it was a test, the child became anxious, nervous, and even hostile, and therefore did much worse on the test. This is because the Black child is only too aware of the uses to which these tests are put by white society. The test has been the main instrument of trying to make Black people believe that they are inferior, and test results are used as an excuse to put Black children in the lowest stream in schools. The Black child knows this only too well. He knows that the test is rigged in advance (by its cultural bias against him) to ensure his failure, and so he abandons all attempts to do well on it. This can be seen most clearly when a group of Black children were told that the results of their tests would be compared with the results obtained from white children. In this case, all the Black children did much worse than when they were told they would be compared with other Black children.

In Britain, Peter Watson,[14] a white Educational Psychologist, went to a secondary school in East London where there are many West Indian pupils. He took with him a Black assistant. The two of them tested groups of West Indian children separately. The group of West Indian children tested by the Black examiner did considerably better than the group tested by Peter Watson, the white examiner. In other words, they did much *worse* under the white examiner than under the Black one. And the difference in scores was even greater than what Professor Katz found in his experiments in America.

What is very significant to note is that these West Indian children, on returning to their classrooms after completing the test with the white examiner, displayed feelings of aggression and anger which the teachers in the classes noticed. But the West Indian children showed no such emotional reaction after being examined by the Black examiner. Professor Katz had the same experience in America, and so did Dr. Baratz.

As Erik Erikson, a world-famous social anthropologist, has pointed out, these IQ tests are influenced by the general state of race relations in the society at the time at which the test is conducted. These tests are not conducted in test-tubes in a laboratory. The child who is doing the test is acutely aware of what white people think about Black people, and how they *treat* Black people. It is no accident that a four-year-old Negro girl in America told Mary Goodman, a psychologist, that: 'The people that are white, they can go up. The people that are brown, they have to go down.'[15] For even a four-year-old Black child understands clearly the role ascribed to Black people by white-dominated society. She knows, even at that age, just how far she can expect to go, socially, economically, and educationally.

The Black child in Britain, facing a white examiner, remembers the white landlord who has pushed Mum and Dad around;

14 P. Watson, 'Race and intelligence', *New Society,* No. 407 (July 16, 1970).

15 M. Goodman, *Race Awareness in Young Children* (1964).

he remembers the face of Powell on the television screen, demanding the repatriation of Black people and their 'picca-ninny' children; he has seen on the news and heard his parents talk about white skinheads and the white police who have beaten up Black people in the streets at night. More than likely he has encountered a racist teacher in the past; he has certainly been called 'Black bastard' or 'Wog' by many of the white chil-dren on more occasions than he cares to remember. If he lives in Haringey, he would almost certainly have heard about Alder-man Doulton of the Haringey Education Committee stating that Black children had achieved significantly lower IQ scores than white children, the inference being that 'something must be done about these Black children'. He might have put two and two together and realised that this is why he sees so many Black children, including some of his friends, going to ESN schools. The thought will not have escaped him that the test he is about to sit before the white examiner, who is an official of white society, will undoubtedly be used against him, as it has been used against so many of his friends.

Under these circumstances, and in this entire racial context, the Black child feels (and quite rightly) that he is fighting a losing battle. He becomes so consumed with fear, inner rage and hatred, that he is unable to think clearly when attempting the test. Under these circumstances, the very bright child does averagely, and the average child does poorly.

❱ Conclusion

The Black child labours under three crucial handicaps:

1 • Low expectations on his part about his likely performance in a white-controlled system of education;

2 • Low motivation to succeed academically because he feels the cards are stacked against him; and finally,

25

3 • Low teacher-expectations which affect the amount of effort expended on his behalf by the teacher, and also affect his own image of himself and his abilities.

If the system is rigged against you and if everyone expects you to fail, the chances are you will expect to fail too. If you expect to fail, the chances are, you will.

CHAPTER 5

What the British School System Does to the Black Child

Some time ago a white boy of thirteen in the school for Educationally Subnormal children where I teach, asked my permission to draw a picture of me. I had been his class teacher for one year. I had a very good relationship with him, and he was very fond of me. He enjoyed drawing. The picture he did of me was quite good. He had included my spectacles, which he always teased me about, and he also drew my moustache and beard while he made great jokes about them. When he was finished, he passed me the paper with the portrait of myself, looking very pleased with himself at having drawn what he considered a near-likeness. I said to him: 'Haven't you forgotten to do something?'

'What?' he said, looking curious and suspicious.

'You forgot to colour my face. My face and cheeks, etcetera, they are not white, are they?'

'No, no! I can't do that!' he said, looking worried.

'Well, you said you were painting a picture of me. Presumably you wanted it to look like me. You painted my hair, moustache and beard, and you painted them black – which they are. So you have to paint my face dark brown if it is to look like me at all.'

'No! I can't. I can't do that. No. No,' he said, looking highly embarrassed and disturbed. He then got up and walked away, finding himself a hammer to do woodwork within the corner of the room far away from me.

This same boy, along with one of his white school friends, had waited outside the school gate for me one afternoon the previous week. When I approached, one of them said: 'People are saying that you are coloured, but you aren't, sir, are you?' This was a rhetorical question on their part. They both looked very worried that 'some people' should be calling me 'coloured', and wanted my reassurance that I was not. They both liked and admired me, and hated thinking that I might be coloured! I explained to them then, as I *had* done many times before in class, that I *was* Black, that I was from the West Indies, and that my forefathers came from Africa. They obviously had mental blocks against accepting me as being Black.

This white boy, who did not even know who 'coloured people' were, obviously had the most fearful image of what Black people were supposed to be like, even though his favourite teacher was Black, and one of his closest friends in class was a Black child. I happened to know that his house-mother at the children's home where he lives has never discussed race with him, and does not display any open prejudice to Black people. In fact, she has, over the years, been an excellent foster-mother to two West Indian boys. Yet he picked up from somewhere a sufficiently adverse image of Black people, that he could not bear to have his favourite teacher be 'coloured', and could not bring himself to draw me as I was – a Black man. He had to have my face white!

This experience of mine gave me an idea: if this is how two white boys in the class felt about me, then perhaps they felt the same way about their close friend, Desmond, a Black boy of eleven from Jamaica. So I gathered together all the drawings and paintings which the children had done of each other, and sure enough, Desmond got painted white by all the white children! What's worse, Desmond and the other four Black children had painted each other white also!

A week later, Desmond, the West Indian boy, asked me to draw a picture of him. I drew the outline, as he watched, making critical comments from time to time. Having completed the outline, I began shading his face black. He immediately said: 'What – what are you doing? You are *spoiling* me!'

I said: 'No, of course not. I am painting you as you are – Black; just like I am. Black is beautiful, you know. You aren't ashamed of that, are you?'

At that he calmed down, and I completed shading his face black. Then I did his hair. His hair was black, short, and very African in texture. I drew it exactly as his hair really was. When he saw it, he jumped out of his chair and shouted: 'You painted me to look like a golliwog! You make me look just like a golliwog!' and he was half about to cry, half about to pounce on me for having done so terrible a thing as to have drawn his hair like it was, instead of making it long, straight and brown, as he had drawn himself in the past!

After I had calmed him down, again by pointing out that my hair was exactly the same as his, and that I liked mine, he decided to retaliate by drawing one of me. He drew my hair black and African-like, he drew my moustache and beard, but he, like the white boy before, refused to shade my face dark brown or black even though I had done his that way. When I asked him to draw my face the colour it really was, rather than leaving it white, he said very emotionally: 'You do it yourself!', and walked out of the room.

Obviously, in an English classroom, it is terrible to be Black. The white child is concerned lest his best friend be considered Black, and the Black child is more than concerned that he should be considered Black!

And this is what this society, with the aid of the school system, is doing to our Black children!

The examples I have given above are not isolated ones. There is the Indian girl in my class who wears Indian clothes to school and whose mother wears her caste-marks and sari when going anywhere, and yet this girl once denied she was Indian when speaking to her English friends in the class. Or there is the case of the Jamaican girl in my class who pretended not to know where Jamaica was, and stated indignantly that she was not from 'there' when speaking to some of the other children one day. Both conversations I overheard by accident. I could give case after case, for they are endless. In fact, none of the West Indian children whom I taught and ran clubs for over a period of three years, have failed to reveal their feelings of ambiguity, ambivalence, and at times despair, at being Black. Many have been made neurotic by their school experience.

❯ How the System Works

The Black child's true identity is denied daily in the classroom. In so far as he is given an identity, it is a false one. He is made to feel inferior in every way. In addition to being told he is dirty and ugly and 'sexually unreliable', he is told by a variety of means that he is intellectually inferior. When he prepares to leave school, and even before, he is made to realise that he and 'his kind' are only fit for manual, menial jobs.

The West Indian child is told on first entering the school that his language is second rate, to say the least. Namely, the only way he knows how to speak, the way he has always communicated with his parents and family and friends; the language in which he has expressed all his emotions, from joy to sorrow; the language of his innermost thoughts and ideas, is 'the wrong way to speak'.

A man's language is part of him. It is his only vehicle for expressing his thoughts and feelings. To say that his language and that of his entire family and culture is second rate, is to accuse him of *being* second rate. But this is what the West Indian child is told in one manner or another on his first day in an English school.

As the weeks and months progress, the Black child discovers that all the great men of history were white – at least, those are the only ones he has been told about. His reading books show him white children and white adults exclusively. He discovers that white horses, white rocks and white unicorns are beautiful and good; but the word 'Black' is reserved for describing the pirates, the thieves, the ugly, the witches, etcetera. This is the *conditioning effect* of what psychologists call *word association* on people's minds. If every reference on TV, radio, newspapers, reading books and story books in school shows 'Black' as being horrible and ugly, and everything 'white' as being pure, clean and beautiful, then people begin to think this way on racial matters.

Several months ago in my class, I was reading one of S.K. McCullagh's story books for children, *The Country of the Red Birds*. This author is world famous, and she has written numerous story books and reading series for children, used in schools in many parts of the world. She is actually a lecturer in psychology. In this story, these two white children went out to the 'island of Golden Sands'. They got to the 'white rock', where the very helpful 'white unicorn' lives. When they met the unicorn, 'the first thing that they saw was a Black ship, with Black sails, sailing towards the white rock'.

'The Black pirates! The Black pirates!' cried the little unicorn. 'They'll kill us! Oh, what shall we do?'

Finally they escaped from the white rock, which the 'Black pirates' had taken over, and went to the island of the 'red birds'. There, 'a Black pirate stood on the sand, with a red bird in his hand', about to kill it. The white boys and the white unicorn, along with the other red birds, managed to beat off the Black pirate, and the red birds in gratitude to the white boys and white unicorn state: 'We will do anything for you, for you have saved a red bird from the Black pirates.'

For those who may be sceptical about the influence of word association on people's minds, it is interesting to note that when I said 'Black pirates' in the story, several of the white children in the class turned their heads and looked at the Black children, who in turn looked acutely embarrassed.

When the pictures, illustrations, music, heroes, great historical and contemporary figures in the classroom are all white, it is difficult for a child to identify with anyone who is not white. When in addition the pictures of Blacks are golliwog stereotypes, about whom filthy jokes are made; when most plays show Black men doing servant jobs; when the word 'Black' in every story book is synonymous with evil, then it becomes impossible for the child to want to be Black. Put another way, it would be unnatural of him not to want to be white. Does this not explain why Desmond and the other Black children draw themselves as white? Can you blame them?

But this not the end of the picture, unfortunately, for the Black children know they are Black. Whenever they might begin in their fantasy to believe otherwise, they are soon reassured on this score by being told they are 'Black bastards' whenever there is a row in the playground – and even when there is not.

The children are therefore made neurotic about their race and culture. Some become behaviour problems as a result. They become resentful and bitter at being told their language is second rate, and their history and culture is non-existent; that they hardly exist at all, except by grace of the whites – and then only as platform sweepers on the Underground, manual workers, and domestic help.

The Black child under these influences develops a deep inferiority complex. He soon loses motivation to succeed academically, since, at best, the learning experience in the classroom is an elaborate irrelevance to his personal life situation, and at worst it is a racially humiliating experience. He discovers in an amazingly short space of time the true role of the Black man in a white-controlled society, and he abandons all intellectual and career goals. Remember the four-year-old Black girl in America, mentioned earlier, who said to Mary Goodman:

'The people that are white, they can go up. The people that are brown, they have to go down.' When two other psychologists in America (Radke and Trager) investigated 'Children's perception of the social roles of Negroes and Whites',[16] the 'poor house' was assigned to Negroes and the 'good house' to Whites by the great majority of white and Negro children aged five to eight years.

❯ Conclusion

The Black child acquires two fundamental attitudes or beliefs as a result of his experiencing the British school system: a low self image, and consequently low self expectations in life. These are obtained through streaming, banding, bussing, ESN schools, racist news media, and a white middle-class curriculum; by totally ignoring the Black child's language, history, culture, identity. Through the choice of teaching materials, the society emphasises who and what it thinks is important – and by implication, by omission, who and what it thinks is unimportant, infinitesimal, irrelevant. Through the belittling, ignoring or denial of a person's identity, one can destroy perhaps the most important aspect of a person's personality – his sense of identity, of who he is. Without this, he will get nowhere.

16 *Journal of Psychology, Vol. 29*, No. 1 (1950), pp. 3-33.

CHAPTER 6

Self-hatred: The Black and White Doll Experiments

The Black child is prepared, both by his general life experiences and by the classroom, for a life of self-contempt. He learns to hate his colour, his race, his culture, and to wish he were white. He learns to consider Black things and Black people as ugly, and white things and white people as beautiful. He believes that since he is Black, he can never be beautiful. Therefore, when he draws a picture of himself, he draws himself white. When he draws *any* picture of a man, it is always that of a white man. Not a single Black child has ever drawn me a picture of a Black man. Of hundreds of drawings done for me over the years by Black children, every one of them is of a white man!

In America, Kenneth B. Clark and Maime P. Clark did a famous study[17] which demonstrates beyond all doubt the Black child's self-contempt. They interviewed a sample of Black children aged three to eight years old from all parts of America. The children were shown two dolls, one Black and the other white. They were first asked to pick 'the doll that looks like a white child'. Ninety-four per cent of the children picked out the right doll. Then they were asked for 'the doll that looks like a coloured child'. Ninety-four per cent got the right doll.

This showed that the vast majority (93 to 94 per cent) understood and could recognise which doll looked like each race.

---

17 'Racial identification and preference in Negro children'. In T.M. Newcomb and T.L. Hartley (eds), *Readings in Social Psychology* (1947), pp. 169-178.

They were then asked to pick the doll that they liked to play with best. *Thirty-two per cent picked the coloured doll, and 67 per cent chose the white doll!*

The Black children were then asked: 'Give me the doll that is a nice doll', and 38 per cent chose the coloured doll, but *59 per cent chose the white doll as the 'nice' doll.*

When they were asked for the doll that looked bad, 59 per cent picked the coloured doll, *and only 17 per cent picked the white doll!*

When asked for the doll that was a 'nice colour' 38 per cent chose the coloured doll and *60 per cent chose the white doll.*

Finally, they were asked: 'Give me the doll that looks like you.' Sixty-six per cent picked the coloured doll, and *33 per cent (one third) of these Black children aged three to eight chose the white doll as the one that looked like them!*

As the Clarks point out with reference to the last question, '...Some of the children who were free and relaxed in the beginning of the experiment broke down and cried or became somewhat negativistic during the latter part when they were required to make self-identifications. Indeed, two children ran out of the testing-room, unconsolable, convulsed in tears.'

In case anyone is liable to dismiss the above evidence on the grounds that this happened in America and does not apply to the West Indian in Britain, I have bad news for you. The same test was conducted in Britain recently, with the same results!

CHAPTER 7

Why our Children get the Worst Education: The Immigrants' Role in Britain

There are two reasons for the presence of Black immigrants in this country:

(a) Our countries have been so successfully fleeced that the only employment opportunities open to a very large section of our people have been in England, where all our stolen wealth resides. Therefore we left the West Indies in search of work.

(b) The British capitalist needed our services, and actively recruited us in the West Indies because of Britain's shortage of unskilled labour, particularly for dirty jobs.

Immigrants in Britain perform four major tasks:

1 • We increase the *supply of labour* through our presence, particularly unskilled labour, relative to the *demand,* thus keeping wages down *and profits up.*

2 • We perform many of the menial and unwanted jobs where otherwise there would be a labour shortage.

3 • We immigrants, without realising it, serve to divide the working class and dampen their militancy. This is because on the one hand, the native worker feels threatened job and social status wise by the arrival of the immigrant and, on the other hand, he moves one rung further up the social

ladder by the presence of immigrants who form *the* lowest social rung. We have the lowest social status because we are given the worst jobs, the worst housing, and we are never accepted by the society. Both because the English worker feels threatened job-wise and because he has, by our presence here, someone to look down on, he adopts a prejudiced and discriminatory position towards us. The incitement to racial hatred adopted by various members of the Establishment, notably Enoch Powell, has the effect of diverting the workers' energies and attention away from the main cause of their low economic position – the Establishment itself.

4 • The Establishment pays cheaply for us in another way apart from wages – in the lack of provision of capital infrastructure, mainly housing, schools, and health and recreational facilities. Both because of low wages and our widespread experience of prejudice, most of us are forced to live in overcrowded, run-down areas, with the least amenities. There is no new provision of housing for our needs, despite our contribution to the economy. Thus, the society gets us as cheaply as possible, to plug a crucial gap in the economy – the need for a sizeable unskilled labour force.[18]

But there are contradictions in the Establishment's position. Through the incitement of prejudice as a diversionary tactic, the white masses have become so insecure that they have demanded the cessation of the flow of immigrants; and many have gone further, following Powell's lead, and suggested the deportation of coloured immigrants. But this is unwelcome to Big Business, which sees in this the danger of losing their cheap

18 For evidence on the economic contribution of the immigrant to the British economy, see K. Jones and A.D. Smith, *Economic Impact of Commonwealth Immigration* (1970). See also Peter Evans, *The Times,* July 17, 1970.

labour market. Thus, all three political parties do nothing to remove the immigrant from Britain. The Guyanese Government has asked the British Government to assist in advertising and financing a programme to encourage Guyanese and other West Indians living in this country to return to Guyana to help in Guyana's development needs. The British Government appears to have done nothing in response.

But there is another threat to Big Business and the social 'order'. If the children of us immigrants were to get equal educational opportunities then, in one generation, there would be no large labour pool from underdeveloped countries prepared to do the menial and unwanted jobs in the economic system, at the lowest wages and in the worst housing; for our children, armed with a good education, would demand the jobs – and the social status that goes with such jobs – befitting their educational qualifications. This would be a very bad blow to Britain's 'social order', with its notions about the right place of the Black man in relation to the white man in society.

Thus, the one way to ensure no changes in the social hierarchy and abundant unskilled labour is to adopt and adapt the educational system to meet the needs of the situation: to prepare our children for the society's future unskilled and ill-paid jobs. It is in this perspective that we can come to appreciate why so many of our Black children are being dumped in ESN schools, secondary moderns,[19] the lowest streams of the comprehensive schools, and 'Bussed' and 'Banded' about the school system.

19 Secondary Moderns were set up essentially for white working-class secondary-age students when universal secondary education was introduced in Britain after World War II.

CHAPTER 8

Conclusions and Recommendations

This booklet has been written for the West Indian community in Britain, though a lot of its message is relevant to the educational problems of Black children in the West Indies and America as well. It is written particularly for West Indian parents, since parents are in a position to do the most for their children, and since West Indian parents are known traditionally for being tremendously sacrificing and ceaselessly ambitious over their children's educational progress and general welfare. It is also written with West Indian teachers, educational psychologists, social workers and community leaders in mind; for through their awareness of the scandalous situation which befalls our children, they can help to galvanise and organise the community for whatever actions are needed to radically alter the situation. The recommendations which follow proceed logically from the evidence presented in this booklet and are in most cases self-evident. They represent the *minimum conditions* which we as a Black community can and will accept for our children.

❱ Recommendations that We as a West Indian Community Must Insist On in Dealing with the Authorities

1 • No West Indian child (or any immigrant child, for that matter) to be placed in an ESN school unless and until he has had a minimum of two years in a normal school.[20]

2 • Moreover, any child considered for placement in an ESN school should receive first a minimum of eighteen months to two years of intensive help in 'opportunity classes' in normal school. 'Opportunity classes' should not be full-time classes, but classes which the child attends for one or two hours each day, to get special help. We do not wish to create ESN 'ghetto' streams within the normal school.

3 • All West Indian children of 65+ IQ, at present in ESN schools, are to be returned promptly to normal schools, where special provisions should be arranged through 'opportunity classes' to return them to normal academic standards. Chapters 2, 3 and 4 demonstrate beyond all reasonable doubt that a West Indian child given a score of 65 on a white, middle-class IQ test, conducted by a white Educational Psychologist or Medical Officer of Health, is undoubtedly in the 80-90 IQ range *at least*. Such children have no right to be in ESN schools.

There is also a need for a re-examination of the placing of large numbers of West Indian children in the lowest streams of secondary schools. Chapter 3 shows conclusively the profound influence of teacher expectations (of which

---

20 As the Little, Mabey and Whittaker study on 'The education of immi-grant pupils in Inner London primary schools' (*Race, Vol. 9*, No. 4 (1968, pp. 439-452) points out in its conclusions: 'There is a consistent and marked improvement in immigrant performance with increasing length of English education.'

streaming is a manifestation) on a child's academic performance.

4 • All remaining West Indian children in ESN schools (in other words, those of 50-65 IQ) should be reassessed by a Black Educational Psychologist at the earliest opportunity, with a view to their referral back to normal schools if this proves justified in their opinion.

5 • A committee of West Indian educationalists should be set up to look into the possibility of standardising the present IQ tests to West Indian cultural requirements, or constructing a test *or other method of assessment* specifically applicable to the West Indian child, whichever seems necessary in the opinion of that body.

6 • In the meantime, all IQ and other tests on West Indian children must be conducted by West Indian Educational Psychologists *only.* (I would humbly suggest the same for Indian and Pakistani children.) Chapter 4 demonstrates, on the basis of experience, the absolute necessity for this.

7 • There should be the recruiting of as many West Indian teachers as possible for schools with large numbers of West Indian children. All 'opportunity classes' should be Black staffed. Chapters 4, 5 and 6 demonstrate the importance of providing our Black children with adults to identify with and feel proud of, to help to break the vicious circle of self-contempt.

8 • Black history and culture, in other words, the history of Black people throughout the Caribbean, the Americas, Africa and Asia, should be made part of the curriculum of *all* schools, for the benefit of the Black *and* the White children. Chapters 5 and 6 demonstrate the urgent necessity for this beyond doubt. Indeed, its exclusion from most school curricula constitutes nothing short of criminal negligence (or prejudice) in the educational sphere.

9 • Parents whose children are being considered for ESN placement should always be informed of what is happening at every stage in the process of assessment, and of their right to object and appeal against any decision. They should be informed of their rights orally and in writing, and the precise nature and purpose of an ESN school should be explained clearly to them, as it affects their child.

❱ Things We Can Do For Ourselves

1 • We need to open Black nursery schools and supplementary schools throughout the areas we live in, in Britain. Our nursery schools should have Black dolls and toys and pictures, and story books about great Black men and women, and their achievements and inventions. Our children need to have a sense of identity, pride, and belonging, as well as mental stimulation, so that they do not end up hating themselves and their race, and being dumped in ESN schools. Pride and self-confidence are the best armour against the prejudice and humiliating experiences which they will certainly face in school and in the society.

We should start up supplementary schools in whatever part of London, or Britain, we live, in order to give our children additional help in the subjects they need. These classes can be held on evenings and Saturday mornings. We should recruit all our Black students and teachers for the task of instructing our children. Through these schools we hope to make up for the inadequacies of the British school system, and for its refusal to teach our children our history and culture. We must never sit idly by while they make ignoramuses of our children, but must see to it that by hook or crook, our children get the best education they are capable of. Some supplementary schools have already been started in parts of London. Do not be the last to get your child in one!

2 • Parents must make it their duty to visit the schools that their children attend *as often as possible*. This will keep the teachers on their toes and make them realise you mean business where the education of your child is concerned. Find out what 'stream' your child is in, and why. If you think he should be doing better, let them know your views. Do not be taken in by the usual statement that, 'Your child is doing all right.' Show them you are concerned with your child's progress, and let the child know that you care about his progress too. The whole point of this booklet is to show you that it is not always or only the child's fault, if he is not succeeding.

3 • We should talk and chat with our children as often as we can. Make the time when necessary. Quite often the child has bad experiences at school, with other children, or with the teacher, or with the sort of work he is being given at school. The only way we can find out about his problems and help him with them is through chatting with him.

4 • We should **read** to our children, especially West Indian story books and books about Black people throughout the world. See the book list at the end of this booklet (Appendix II) for the sort of books you can read with your children. The book list also has the name and address of the West Indian bookshop where all these books can be obtained.

5 • Toys such as bricks and other playing materials are very **important** to provide our small children with. Psychologists

43

have proved beyond all doubt that they help to make children more active mentally and think better. If they get bricks, puzzles, drawing and colouring books, as well as dolls and small cars to play with from the time they are one year up, they will tend to be *much* brighter when they start school. (And if we do not want them to hate themselves, we must get them **Black** dolls. Remember Chapter 6?)

6 • Finally, if you are a West Indian parent with a child at an ESN school, read over this booklet carefully, take it and show it to the head teacher at the school, and go and see the Chief Education Officer of your borough and demand a reassessment of your child by a Black Educational Psychologist, in the light of this booklet.

CHAPTER 9

Questions and Answers for Parents

❯ What is an ESN Special School? What type of child does it cater for?

Once they were called 'feeble-minded', then 'mentally subnormal', and now the children are called 'Educationally Subnormal' or 'ESN' for short. As Chapter 1 demonstrates, ESN schools are really for children who are naturally of very low intelligence. They are *not* remedial schools in the sense of preparing the child for return to normal school. They keep children on a permanent basis. They do *not* therefore cater properly for the child who is of normal intelligence but functioning badly because of language or emotional difficulties, or because he has missed a lot of schooling before coming to this country. In fact, there is some evidence that such children deteriorate mentally at ESN schools.

❯ How and why do children get sent there?

Usually, the child's class teacher makes a report to the head teacher, to the effect that the child is far behind in his work, does not seem to be catching up, and seems dull. Quite often the real truth is that the child may be giving trouble to the teacher – being a 'bloody nuisance' – and this is one way of the teacher, and the school, being rid of him. Quite often the child may be going through a difficult patch of emotional disturbance, when he cannot concentrate on his studies, and this is confused with his intelligence.

The head teacher then makes a report to the education authorities, and then the Medical Officer of Health arranges a medical examination and an IQ test of the child. The Medical Officer of Health then decides, in some boroughs on his own (!), in other boroughs with the help of the headmaster and an Educational Psychologist, whether the child should be sent to an ESN school.

❯ What is an IQ test?

An IQ test is a test conducted by a Medical Officer of Health or Educational Psychologist intended to measure the intelligence of a child. It consists of a series of questions (many of them quite stupid, and unrelated to the experiences of West Indian children; see Chapter 2) and tasks for the child to do, lasting about one hour. If the child is upset, emotionally disturbed, unable to understand what the Educational Psychologist is saying, or if the child is uneasy because of never having done a test like this before, then the score or 'marks' which the child will get on the test will have nothing whatever to do with his real intelligence. This is why the test is so absurd and very harmful when given to West Indian children, particularly those with difficulties. West Indian children feel more at ease and do considerably better on the tests when they are conducted by West Indian Educational Psychologists, so always insist on one if they want to test your child.

❯ Do parents have any say over whether their child is placed in an ESN school? Can parents refuse? Can they appeal against any decision?

Parents must be consulted before a child can be given a medical examination and IQ test. Parents must be consulted, also, if a decision to send their child to an ESN 'Special' school is taken. If parents insist that the child be given remedial help in the normal school instead of ESN placement, then many authorities will probably agree. However, they can refuse, and place your child in an ESN school even if you object. In such a case, *you have the right of appeal.* If you can bring evidence and arguments to support your case, then the Borough Education Committee or the Secretary of State for Education *might* reverse the decision. But they have the last word. If you think your child is being wrongly placed, then it is always worth your while to protest and appeal. It might force them to think again.

▶ Can a child be transferred back from an ESN school to a normal school?

Yes. But this happens very rarely (see Chapter 1). The only cases I know of were cases where the parents kept on putting pressure on the headmaster and the school.

▶ What is the alternative to ESN school for a child of normal ability but who is doing badly at school?

Remedial or 'opportunity' classes in the normal school. These are classes (which only some boroughs have – and you should press your borough to start them if they have not) where the child can have an hour or two of special help in the subjects he needs help in (like English and Arithmetic) from a well-qualified and experienced teacher. West Indian children tend to do much better when taught by West Indian teachers, so you must make it your duty to press your education authority to hire more Black teachers for your child's sake.

Notes...

PART 2

Why I Wrote the 'ESN Book': 30 Years On

Notes ...

The Backdrop

© Bernard Coard 2004
PREVIOUSLY PUBLISHED IN *THE GUARDIAN*,
5 FEBRUARY 2005

❯❯ The Issues Facing Black Children 30 to 40 Years Ago

Written over three decades ago, my small book was an attempt to explore with Black parents and the Black community generally, some of the reasons for the abysmal failure of their children within the British school system. These included:

> ❯ The racist policies and practices of the education authorities of that period;

> ❯ Racism within the curriculum itself; the actual reading materials which the children were obliged to use.

> ❯ The poor self-image, self-esteem, self-belief which the vast majority of the Black children experienced; some of the reasons for this, and its consequences for their school (and later life) performance.

> ❯ Low teacher expectations, and how destructive a force this could be.

> ❯ Inadequate Black parental knowledge of and involvement in what was happening to their children at school in that period.

> The lack of Black parental organisation to tackle the situation faced by their children; including especially the need for more Black teachers in the schools, and the need to set up Black supplementary schools in the Black community.

The focus, then, was quite naturally on the so-called schools for the educationally subnormal (ESN); schools which, incidentally, were previously officially called schools for the mentally subnormal (MSN). These schools were being utilised by the education authorities as a dumping ground for Black children. This was especially so for those who had recently come from the Caribbean to join their parents; often after a separation of several years.

These children were therefore encountering various degrees of emotional disturbance; on top of the normal cultural and other adjustment problems associated with a sudden move to an entirely new environment. The response of the authorities was not one of addressing their difficulties and needs, but of branding many of them as 'educationally subnormal', and then dispatching them to ESN schools.

The issues raised in the book, however, applied to the plight of Black children throughout the British school system, and not just to those sent to ESN schools. Racist policies, racist curricula, problems of low self-esteem and low teacher expectations, and so on, infected the entire school system. This had devastating consequences for the overall performance of Black children throughout Britain. Yes, many Black children 'made it' academically in that period of the late 1960s and 70s despite all the odds. Those children are, by and large, today's highly successful adult Blacks. However, the vast majority were not so lucky.

❱ The Children the Book Spoke Of Are the Parents and Grandparents of Today's Children

What is particularly important to note is that the children of the 1960s and 1970s whom the British education system failed are the parents and grandparents of today's children – large numbers of whom are being suspended and 'excluded' from schools, or placed in 'special units' or streams. For many reasons true then as now, Black boys were affected far more than Black girls. The lesson to be learned for today's problems in the school system is that they were 'hatched' decades ago, in the previous two generations. When society fails one generation of children, it lays the foundations for similar, even worse failures in the generations to follow. We human beings 'inherit' not only through our genes, but often also from our social circumstances.

Those in charge of the education system have chosen not to seriously address and solve the problems. Instead, they have shifted around the problem; even sought to hide it from view. Yes, they (eventually) closed down the ESN schools. But they found other ways to shunt Black children with educational difficulties (emotional, cultural, medical, and so on) into a corner and essentially ignore their needs – and potential – rather than put the resources needed into addressing them.

Disguised (and not so disguised) forms of streaming have emerged to specially deal with these 'difficult' Black children. As the kids' frustration levels have risen and the number becoming disruptive, even violent, have grown, the tactic of 'exclusion' (even for the non-violent in many cases) has become a regular tool for getting rid of, rather than tackling the children's problems.

The growing numbers of children and young people resorting to violence in schools has created a serious problem for many teachers. This reflects on the system as a whole, rather than on the teachers, who are experiencing the results of the neglect of past decades as well as the reality of today's racism in so many areas of the children and their parents' lives. It must never be forgotten, however, that no child was born violent. To merely throw these children out of school not only solves nothing; it ensures worse violence in the future. The suspension and expulsion of kids – disproportionately Black kids – from school because of misbehaviour (of various sorts and gravity) does not solve society's – or these youths' – problems, but postpones, while making worse, the day of society's reckoning for having failed to educate and cherish these youths when they were younger. And let us not forget that these 'excluded' youths will be the parents, one day, of children themselves. This reality tells us that if we are to make a real difference to future generations of Black children, we must start now, with the present generation, to turn things around.

Perhaps this accounts for the long-lasting impact which many have told me my book has had – although I suspect that most simply wished to be kind.

❯ The Objective Reasons for the Timing of the Book

This book, however, could only have been written when it was (during the summer of 1970; published in May 1971) because of the presence, for the first time in British history, of large and growing numbers of Black children in British schools in the 1960s and early 1970s. This, in turn, was a product of the presence, also for the first time in British history, of large and growing numbers of Black immigrants from Britain's colonies and former colonies.

Black people, of course, had lived in Britain for centuries, most of them living in port cities linked to the slave trade. Their numbers, however, were minuscule, and they therefore had little sociological, economic or political impact within British society. In contrast, the Black immigrants of the post-Second World War era had greater impact, as they were both more sizable in number and tended to be concentrated in many of Britain's major cities.

This is because they – [the Windrush generation, as they would come to be widely known[21] after the first recorded ship which brought early batches to Britain] – had been aggressively recruited by both Conservative and Labour governments to fill the massive labour shortages for the lower paid jobs within the British economy, most especially in the transportation, health care, and older, less efficient, relatively labour intensive factories throughout Britain.

Although the vast majority of the immigrants arrived during the 1950s and the early 1960s, their children became a significant presence in the school system only in the 1960s and beyond. This is because those who already had children at home prior to their migrating to Britain, took a few years to settle – get a job, build up savings, purchase a house – before sending for their children.

Others started families after arriving in Britain, and this also meant a gap of several years before such children would reach school age. This is probably why the book was written when it was and not before or later. But why me? I was not a migrant to Britain, and economics, not education, was my field. Despite this, a combination of factors led me to this book.

---

21 Since the breaking of another scandal in 2018.

The Book

❱ How I Came to Write the Book

I came to Britain in September of 1966 to do a masters degree at Sussex University. When I completed it in the summer of 1967, I started working full-time while signing up for a PhD in development economics at Sussex part-time. My focus was on completing my PhD and returning to the Caribbean to serve my people there.

For the three and a half years between the summer of 1967, when I first started working, and December 1970, I first ran evening clubs for children from seven schools for the 'educationally subnormal' (ESN), and then taught full-time at two other ESN schools. This gave me first-hand experience of what was happening not just in these schools, but in the education system as a whole, as I discovered that the system was using the ESN schools as a convenient dumping ground for Black children who were anything *but* 'educationally subnormal'.

I was outraged by what I was witnessing, but I had no overall data, and therefore no proof, that what I was witnessing in the nine ESN schools to which I was exposed was true throughout the system, or that those in authority knew exactly what was happening and took a conscious decision to do nothing about it.

One day, around the spring of 1970, out of the blue, a cousin of mine contacted me and placed an 'internal' Inner London

56

Education Authority (ILEA) report on all the ESN schools under its jurisdiction into my hands. A friend of hers who worked within the system had clearly decided that enough was enough, and was seeking to get someone, anyone, to take this report with all the tables of statistics and expose and explain its scandalous contents to the public at large. I now had the personal experience, and the hard evidence, of the scandal affecting Black children in the school system.

But I was not a journalist, I had no contacts in the British media; neither was I a member of any organisation – West Indian or otherwise – in Britain. Indeed, I was in Britain for only about 40 months when my cousin placed that 'internal' ILEA report in my lap in the spring of 1970. The questions I asked myself were: 'How do I go about doing something about this scandalous situation? What can I do, concretely, to get people's attention in a really big way, so as to have the situation addressed?'

Just as I was stumped for an answer, I went to a party one Saturday night thrown by six Grenadian friends of mine who shared a house in Tulse Hill. At this party, there where West Indians from all the islands. They had been living in Britain for many years, had children in the school system, and had been 'hearing rumours', as they put it to me, of what was happening in the schools, most especially the ESN ones. More than one came up to me and said, something like, 'We hear you are a teacher [there were precious few Black teachers in those days] in the ESN schools. We are hearing all kinds of things. What's really happening there?'

I explained as best as I could what was 'happening'. By the end of the evening, I was asked by several of those present to prepare and present a paper on the situation to a conference which was to be held a few weeks later. Samuel Selvon, Andrew Salkey, and other West Indian literary greats were also due to be presenting papers, I was told. By sheer 'accident' – or divine will – I had found a vehicle to get the message into the Black community. But would a few dozen parent-activists from the community be enough? Time alone would tell.

After I presented my paper to the many dozens of West Indian community activists who were present, a lively question-and-answer and then general discussion followed. At the end of it all, I was virtually ordered by all present to turn that paper into a book. I was given, in practice, a deadline of three months to write the book, as everyone was anxious to have the scandal exposed in the shortest possible time.

I set to work on the book, using the three summer months of 1970 when there was no school, and no classes at Sussex for me to attend. I spent each day in London University's School of Education library, and each night collating my voluminous notes and drafting chapters. By the time the summer was over, I had written 210 typewritten pages, outlining the many problems Black children were facing, why, and what I felt should be done about them.

I then took a critical decision. I would address the book explicitly to Black parents. Not to teachers, not to the education and political authorities, not to the public at large; exclusively to Black parents. I wanted to get them conscious of the problems, and organised to deal with them. I wanted them to feel personally spoken to; to recognise that this was a problem that they had to get up and tackle; not rely on any others to do on their behalf.

I wanted a book written for them, and addressed directly to them. This decision meant that I could not take the approach of writing an academic treatise on the education of Black children in Britain. Black parents were (still are!) very hardworking and busy people. They didn't have the time to read 210 pages. I would have to concentrate on the most important issues.

Having completed a scaled-down version, I brought the completed manuscript to the leaders of various West Indian organisations for them to have a look at it. They were all satisfied with its contents. Everyone's concern now turned to having it published. We approached all the leading publishers. None would have it. There were two major problems with it from a business standpoint: having never published anything before, my name had no recognition in the educational books market; and I was choosing to write a book for a highly restricted target market – West Indian parents. A tiny fraction of the British population, and one, moreover, which hardly ever bought books.

This response from the established publishing industry, combined with the sense of desperate urgency on the part of the West Indian community leaders, led to them organising a meeting of the leaders of 26 different West Indian community groups and organisations. At this meeting, they took a decision to raise the up-front money to pay a printer and publish the book. A one-man West Indian publishing company, New Beacon Books, headed by the visionary and activist, John LaRose, undertook to have it published; ably supported by another one-person West Indian publishing concern, Bogle L'Ouverture Publications, headed by the indefatigable and visionary Jessica Huntley. The leading West Indian community activist of Hackney at the time, Jeff Crawford, and the late, great Jamaican novelist, Andrew Salkey, lent their support and encouragement throughout, as did many others.

It is one thing to have the necessary facts and evidence to write a book, another to write it, and yet another to raise all the funds to have it published when none of the established publishers would touch it. But there was still one vital piece missing: how were we to distribute – in other words, sell – our 10,000 copies? Every single established distribution chain refused to carry even one copy of the book. We approached them all, and all refused. Their reasoning was essentially the same as that of the big publishers: no author name-recognition, and close to zero market potential. Significantly, when the first print-run was sold out (with the same 26 West Indian organisations pitching in to sell the book door to door in the Black community) in short order, ten different publishers, nine British and one American, approached me to write books on education for them (I now had name-recognition!). And suddenly, the leading book distribution chain of that era got in touch with me, offering to now sell the book. I had the satisfaction of informing them that we needed them no more, as all the copies had been sold out, and a reprint was under serious consideration.

There are two more interesting aspects of the history of how this book came to be. One had to do with how we managed to get the enormous amount of publicity that we did get from the day of publication, and the other to do with how 'the establishment' reacted to the book's publication, and its attendant publicity.

❯ How Do We Publicise the Book and Its Contents?

We owe three Americans all the credit for the extraordinary publicity we were able to generate with respect to the book's contents. The first two, Jim and Carol Bergman, made their invaluable contribution by not just giving me maximum encouragement, but by putting me in touch with the third American, the one who made her living, full-time, as a media consultant. Through their close friendship with her, they got her to agree to advise me fully on how to proceed, free of charge. The 'trade secrets' which she taught me then, for the purposes of launching the book with a blaze of positive publicity, I have taught to all my small business course students in the Caribbean ever since.

This lady let me have her list of 1,400 newspapers and radio and TV programmes, and the names and addresses and phone numbers of all the key news journalists, and columnists, on each of them. She taught me the right colours of paper to print press releases, the size of print, and the size of the margins;

and what information to put in the very first sentence, and first paragraph, of the press release. And so on and so forth. It was the most extraordinary free lesson I ever received in my life.

I put her advice to work, and we had every single paper cover the story positively and accurately in its news and in many of its columns. Every talk show on all the radio and TV stations covered it; usually inviting me to come and be interviewed at some length. The first six minutes of prime time television news on the first day of publication had me debate the facts outlined in the book with the then chief education officer of the ILEA.

That turned out to be a stunning PR coup, as a very sizeable percentage of the British population watched that news programme each day. BBC then did a series of documentaries relevant to the issue of the education of Black children in British schools, and *The Guardian* sought permission and published the whole of Chapter Five of the book on its editorial page. We could not have asked for greater publicity, not to mention highly favourable and generally very accurate publicity, regarding the scandalous data we were seeking to highlight.

❱ The 'Establishment' Responds

The reaction of the 'establishment' took two forms. The first was to rush out their spokespersons to deny everything. At first, they said on radio and TV that the book was 'a pack of lies'. Within days, based on the feedback they were getting, and the fact that I would read directly from their 'internal' report on the electronic media, they amended their position to: 'There is some truth in it, but most of it consists of lies'. By the third week of sustained publicity following the book's publication, they had moved to say 'most of it contains some truth, but there are many untruths too'. By the end of six months following publication, they had surrendered. It was now acknowledged to be 'accurate', and was now 'recommended reading' at teachers colleges and schools of education in many parts of the country!

The other aspect of 'the establishment's' reaction was Big Brother-like. My phone was tapped by the first night of publication. My wife and I were sometimes followed by (presumably) security personnel. Finally, our 11-year-old nephew, who was spending his holidays with us, was harassed by police in a police car close to where we lived and in our presence (deliberately so). My nephew was even threatened with a trumped up charge, with the sergeant in charge all the time looking pointedly into my eyes, seeking to gauge my reaction and clearly trying to send me a message: if you think you are a tough guy, we can always pick on your 11-year-old nephew to whip you into line.

Significantly, around the same time (approximately six months after publication) that the educational establishment backed down on its campaign of vilification of the book, my telephone ceased being tapped, my wife, nephew, and I stopped being followed, and there were no further threats from the police.

❯ The Book's Impact

The Black community's response to the book was incredible. Thousands of Black parents in small groups throughout the country began meeting, and several parents' groups were formed. Black supplementary schools were formed up and down the country. Some estimates put the number of these schools at as many as 150. Black youth groups were formed, and existing ones held regular discussions on the scandal and what their members could do to help. I found myself invited to come and address many of these groups and other organisations all over Britain. From May to September of 1971, I was addressing between three and five such groups each weekday afternoon and evening, and on weekends. The level of concern, and the sheer energy of the participants, was something to behold. Amazingly, several of these groups, and even supplementary schools, survive to this day, 33 years later.

In addition to the extraordinary galvanising effect that the book had within the Black community, it is my belief that the turn-around in the establishment's response also owed a great deal to the support which the contents of the book, its main thrust and objectives, received from thousands of teachers – white teachers, including several head teachers – up and down the country. Significant sections of mainstream British public opinion embraced the fact that what was happening was unfair; indeed scandalous, and should be acknowledged by those in charge and brought to an end. Dozens of journalists went out of their way, too, to get this message across. A book which was written for and intended, by the author, only for Black parents and the Black community, had taken on a life of its own; mobilising, as never before, the Black community, but also reaching, touching, and influencing white teachers, student teachers, university students, journalists, trade union leaders, and other broadly progressive sections of the majority population.

All the above developments forced a rethink and a radical adjustment in tactics on the part of the establishment. They would have to concede, to surrender, on 'this ESN thing', but find new ways of still denying Black children equal and high quality education. We won that battle. Hands down. And we enlisted many persons in the wider society. But, truth be told, Black parents and their children – and white working class ones as well – are yet to win the war. Indeed, they are as far away from winning it as ever before, except for a minority of Black people, who have been fortunate to 'make it' educationally and otherwise.

Thirty Years On: Where Do We Go From Here?

PREVIOUSLY PUBLISHED IN *THE GUARDIAN*, 5 FEBRUARY 2005

❯ High Quality Education for All

It is to that wider war – a war whose slogan and rallying cry, I suggest, should be 'High quality education for all!' – that all should address their minds, and focus their organising energies to achieve. It is my belief, backed up by recent relevant research from the US, that a successful assault on poverty, racism, gender and class discrimination, and on the income, wealth, social status and decision-making gaps which go with these in British society, requires a fundamental transformation of the British education system. It is not that the transformation of the education system will, by itself, solve all these other problems. But it would be the decisive foundation from which all these other problems can be effectively addressed. It would empower entire future generations with the tools, the resources, the ability, to tackle these other vital societal ills. Moreover, the process of transforming the education system will itself throw up forces which will be critical in addressing these other ills.

❯ Education as the Most Important Form of Wealth for Families and Nations

Discriminatory education is a critical factor in the maintenance of income and wealth inequality in any society. Equally, the provision of quality education for the poor and the marginalised in society is critical to the closing, over time and along with other measures, of the income and wealth gaps. It is the key to ending poverty; persistent, generational (in other words, socially inherited) poverty. It is also critical to the acquisition and maintenance of – or exclusion from – such societal 'resources' as status and power within the society; and to social mobility in general.

It is also at a national level, the decisive factor in achieving labour competitiveness in the face of globalisation. (Not a labour competitiveness born of low wages and oppressive working conditions, but one based on high skills, high productivity, and hence high wages.)

Wealth takes many forms. Perhaps its most important form is education. The academic and technical level and skills of a people constitutes the most important 'wealth' of the nation. When the German and Japanese economies – their factories, ports, railways, power plants; in fact, virtually their entire infrastructure and productive capacity – were destroyed during World War II, it took both countries less than 25 years to not only rebound but become the most powerful economies in the world after the US economy. While all their material wealth had been destroyed, their people retained in their heads the scientific and technological knowledge, skills, and experience necessary to restore that material wealth – and more – in relatively little time. What is true at the level of the nation state is also true at the class, ethnic and individual family levels. For example, a well-off family which loses all its material possessions in a fire or other major disaster, and which, for the sake of argument, has no insurance cover, can, over time, rebuild or restore its relatively privileged material position, once its members are highly educated or skilled. The latter (high level of education) can be translated into the former (material wealth). But a family which starts with close to nothing and which, moreover, has little education, will simply sink even lower in the societal totem pole if faced with a disaster which wipes out the little that it has.

❱ Discriminatory Education as a Tool of Subjugation

Discriminatory provision of education to different classes or ethnic or other groups within a society is therefore the single most powerful tool for subjugating, and marginalising those who are denied any, or inferior, education. In this context, it is no accident that, when women were most powerless in societies worldwide, they were denied access to schools. In recent times, we have seen this with the Taliban in Afghanistan.

The discriminatory provision of education for Black people under apartheid in South Africa and in the southern United States in the pre-civil rights era, was linked inextricably to the conscious, official policy of white subjugation of Black people in those societies. Likewise, the fact that universal secondary education was only introduced in Britain half-way through the 20th century (with the 1944 Education Act), while schools for the children of the upper class had existed for centuries, tells its own story.

Moreover, the fierce battle waged by the privileged in Britain in the 1950s, '60s and '70s against the Labour policy of phasing out the heavily class-based system of grammar and secondary modern schools, and replacing them with one type of secondary school (the comprehensive), signals just how important a societal resource education was seen to be by Britain's traditional rulers – as also by that generation of Labour party leaders.

❱ Income, Wealth, Power, Prestige – and Education

The many public debates about – and the condemnation of – those prominent white and Black Labour party leaders who have gone to great financial lengths to send their children to high-quality-education private schools, emphasises just how important those very clever persons (and the upper and middle classes, generally) see education for their children. They perceive it as critical in terms of:

> ❱ Achieving and/or maintaining the family's access to high income, and to wealth creation opportunities.

> ❱ Access to power and high status within the society (whether in government, business, the armed forces, the churches).

> ❱ Strengthening or increasing the family's income/wealth/ power/status ('societal resources') with each new generation of the family.

These clever and highly successful people recognise that rises and falls in access to society's resources (income, wealth, power, prestige) by different generations of the same families are overwhelmingly a factor of education: maintaining – and increasing – each generation's access to education, in relation to that of previous generations; and in particular in relation to that of others in the same generation within the society.

I believe that it is a distraction for progressive people to condemn and vilify those individuals who opt for the best education they can access for their children. Given the centrality of education for accessing and enjoying all of the society's other resources, everyone must instead face squarely and honestly the fundamental structural problem which characterises the education system in order to seek to change it. Its discriminatory provision of educational resources to children and young people, linked to its two-tiered structure; one for those who can afford it privately, and one for the remainder of the society, constitutes the essence of the problem. The growing differentiation in the quality of education provided within the state system further complicates the situation, and widens further the disparities and inequalities which are also manifested in other areas of the society.

❱ 'Donkey Say the World Ent Level'

Children in Britain do not begin life from a level playing field, nor therefore do they enter school for the first time on an equal footing with all their fellow children-citizens of the country. As the old people in the Caribbean like to put it: 'Donkey say the world ent level.' Discriminatory access to jobs, promotion, housing, education, and other societal resources by their parents based on considerations of class, gender, race, and other factors, ensures that each child begins life, and school, with different degrees of 'handicap'.

They start life, and school, with different expectations, differing degrees of self-confidence and self-belief, and different language and other skills. Most critically, they begin with different amounts of financial resources and 'old boy network' resources at their parent's command. Moreover, the schools which exist demand very different degrees of these resources, in order to gain access to them.

❱ Education Earns Money, Which Buys Education, Which Earns Money, Which Buys Education...

To summarise the above, we can say, therefore, that differential access to educational resources leads to differential access to society's other resources, particularly income, wealth, and valuable social contacts and connections. These other societal resources, in turn help to perpetuate inequalities in access to educational resources, since the better off and better 'connected' tend to get the overwhelming majority of the places available at the highest-quality (and usually high fee-paying) educational establishments – thus ensuring vastly different levels of educational achievement by the children of the succeeding generation, and hence differential access by them to income, wealth, power and prestige... and so and so on, from one generation to the next.

Significantly, most of the limited social mobility which occurs within this self-perpetuating and fairly rigid class/race structure has come about through scholarships offered to a tiny percentage of the disadvantaged in each generation. In other words, these few children or young people were privileged to get into the quality-education tier of the education system without the normal requirement for their parents to dish out substantial sums for fees, etcetera – sums which, of course, they would not have had. The nexus between income/wealth and quality-education provision was broken just for these few!

⟩ Break the Link Between Money and Connections, Race and Education

What is needed, instead, is a system of quality education for all, and therefore, by definition, one which is not dependent on the parental wealth, social status and connections; one which does not have schools providing vastly different standards of education; and one which does not have a multi-tiered system of education, providing differential education for the children of different classes, genders and ethnicities. Let us be clear about one thing: the goal is not 'equality of provision of educational resources for all'. If this were the goal, it could be achieved by 'dumbing down' the excellent private schools and the better state schools to the lower standards of the many inadequately resourced state schools. Rather, the goal is 'high quality education for all'. This would require not a lowering of the standards of the best schools but rather a raising of the standards of other schools to that of the best ones. It would

mean undertaking the necessary steps to bring all schools up to
the highest standards.

❯ The Cost and the Benefits of High Quality Education
for All

Some may ask whether the nation has sufficient resources to
spend so as to bring all schools throughout the country up to
high educational standards so that all children can enjoy expo-
sure to these standards. The answer is an unqualified yes.
Britain is a wealthy country with more than sufficient resources
to do this. It is all a question of priorities. Just consider the
enormous sums being spent on nuclear weapons, and on
submarine delivery systems for their use; or what has already
been spent on the Iraq war, and the answer becomes clear.

However, there is another and perhaps even more important answer to the question as to whether the nation has
the necessary resources to transform all its schools into top-
notch learning centres. The answer is that it has no choice, if
it wishes to remain one of the leading economies in today's
highly competitive, knowledge-intensive, globalised environment. The short-sighted approach to competing globally in
today's cut-throat world is to restrict trade unions, dampen
wage increases, slash welfare benefits, reduce workers' fringe
and other benefits, lay off full-time workers and produce more
with part-time, socially unprotected workers, and generally to
introduce what is euphemistically called a 'more flexible labour
force'. The real solution is to transform Britain's working population from being a labour force, into human capital, through
massive investment in education. It is to develop all of Britain's
brainpower to the maximum so that Britain becomes amongst
the most competitive in today's world.

It is important for us to understand the world we are living in
today, for the kind of education system that is needed depends on
our understanding this. In the pre-industrial age, the economy

was labour-intensive. During the heyday of the industrial era, the economy was transformed from being labour-intensive to being capital-intensive. In today's post-industrial, globalised economy, the most successful economies are knowledge-intensive. Nowadays, when you buy a calculator, a mobile phone, or a watch, the plastic and other cheap materials from which these are made represent a tiny fraction of the production costs (and hence price) of these items.

It is the 'brain-labour' of hundreds, sometimes thousands of scientists and technicians which is captured in the extraordinary range of things that these small and 'simple' devices can perform, that accounts for most of the costs of production, and which earn the companies producing them billions of dollars, and the scientists and technicians who designed their software very high salaries. It is generally not recognised that it is computer software, not computer hardware, where the highest profits – and the highest wages – are earned. Making the physical parts of a computer takes relatively old production methods. However, designing the computer software to work within the physical equipment which constitutes the computer itself, takes hundreds of thousands of high-priced brain power. For this reason, it is no accident that starting salaries for computer programmers are so high worldwide.

Indeed, it has been widely reported that virtually all of Microsoft's staff who have been there from the software company's start-up are millionaires and many are multi-millionaires. That is where high productivity, high wage, high profits, and high national income are to be found: in knowledge-intensive industries. In industries utilising highly developed brainpower in the production of goods and services. The more such industries a country has, the more wealthy and competitive the country. In turn, to have such a labour force – sorry, to have such a human capital force – requires the transformation of the education system from its present semi-feudal discriminatory system which fails to fully develop the brainpower and talents

71

of the majority of its children and students – in other words, tomorrow's working population: tomorrow's 'working capital' – into a unified, quality-education-for-all system.

In today's highly competitive, globalised, knowledge-intensive-production world, therefore, the way to equality is the possession of high skills, highly marketable knowledge. The present trends in the education system are geared not just to maintaining centuries-old inequalities and discriminatory treatment, but actually to worsening the class and race chasms which exist. In such an environment, a few Blacks, like a few working class whites, will rise within the system, based on a combination of fortuitous circumstances and ability. But the vast majority of Black and white working class children will not and cannot 'make it' within this class and race-riven system.

All people and organisations of goodwill and good intentions will need, of necessity, to focus their thoughts and energies on uniting in the great battle needed to radically transform the British education system into one of high quality education for all.

❯ Is There a Role for Trade Unions in This Fight?

Yes, this is a task for all trade unions. Trade unions can fight in traditional ways for better wages and working conditions for their present members. True. But what is the best way to fight for future 'better wages and working conditions' for the children of their current members? Through a struggle for root and branch change in the education system so as to genuinely offer equality of educational opportunity for all. This is a battle, then, for parents – Black and white, for teachers, community leaders, church leaders, women and youth groups, student bodies, and the trade union movement.

❱ Should Black People Fight by Themselves, or Form Alliances?

Black supplementary schools, and Black parents, youth, and community groups, remain vital organs in the struggle for high quality education for all Black children. These many organisations in the Black community must be strengthened and many more formed where there are few or none. No victory is possible without struggle, and no struggle can be won without being organised. However, Black people, and their organisations, fighting by themselves, in isolation from other forces which have common aims, will not get far.

This is because Black people are a small minority of the population. If the majority of whites (in other words, the white working mothers and fathers) are having difficulty getting the system to work in their interest, what chance is there for a small minority fighting its battles in isolation from natural allies? Yes, some individual battles may be won in relative isolation. But, to win the war of educational transformation – and hence of poverty elimination and defeat of racism and other ills – we must put sectarianism aside, and join forces with all who have the same goals of an end to discrimination, and the establishment of high-quality schools for all children regardless of class, race, gender, religious or economic circumstances. If all adopt this approach and organise and fight in a focused way for it, victory becomes possible; victory will be achieved!

Notes...

PART 3

50 Years On

Notes ...

'How the West Indian child is made educationally sub-normal in the British school system':

50 Years On[22]

by Professor Emeritus Hubert Devonish

❯ Who is the 'West Indian Child'?

An important feature of a classic work is that it melts into the culture and intellectual tradition of a community through being quoted and referred to second and third hand. Everyone 'knows' the work though they have never read it. That was me when, on 15th December 2020, I agreed to proofread a scanned version of Bernard Coard's 1971 work to help prepare it for publication. As I began to read, I kept being troubled by a question. Who was this 'West Indian child' that is being made educationally sub-normal? The answer seemed obvious. It became less so on a careful examination of the language of the text.

Bernard Coard, hereafter 'BC', uses the male form 'he' in the text to refer to any human being male or female. This generic use of the masculine was common and indeed accepted practice at the time. Just to be clear, I asked BC about how many Caribbean males versus females there were in the ESN schools where he worked. He thought a bit and said that at the first ESN school he was attached to, he worked with one Caribbean male and one Caribbean female pupil. He added, however, that

22 Acknowledging with thanks the substantial contribution of Ewart Thomas to pruning and organising a very unruly original draft.

all the Caribbean pupils that he later encountered in other ESN schools were male.

The statistics he gives in the work are not separated according to gender. In the decades since, the under-performance of male pupils of Caribbean descent in Britain has become a matter of community and public concern. This is not just about how well they do relative to what would be considered normal, but in relation to their female counterparts as well. BC's generic use of 'he', combined with the silence of the statistics he used on the gender issue, disguised the combination of race and gender affecting the Caribbean school population he was studying.

In this work, the term 'West Indian' also seems to bear some hidden meanings. It appears in the main part of the title of the book as 'How the West Indian child is made educationally sub-normal in the British school system'. This was followed by the subtitle 'The scandal of the Black child in schools in Britain'. The subtitle 'Black' was used with the same meaning as 'West Indian'. This is the main way it is used throughout the work even though there are times when 'Black' is employed in the generic sense. We see this when the author enjoins Black parents to read books to their children '...about Black people throughout the world'. Putting aside this exceptional example, the use of 'Black' as a synonym for 'West Indian' is the norm in the work. This can be seen when BC makes proposals for options to ESN schools, stating, 'West Indian children tend to do much better when taught by West Indian teachers, so you must make it your duty to press your education authority to hire more Black teachers for your child's sake.'

Once 'Black' is interpreted in the above quote as referring to people of African descent, 'West Indian' cannot be used as a label for all children from the then or former British possessions in the Caribbean. It is certainly not being used in any conscious way to include the significant number of immigrants to Britain of Indian/South Asian descent, referred to in the Caribbean as 'East Indian'. This sub-group of Caribbean immigrants would have come mainly from Trinidad & Tobago and Guyana where people of Indian descent are about the same in number as or more numerous than those of African descent.

As part of preparing this essay, '50 years on…', I asked BC about his use of 'West Indian' in the work. He reflected that in the schools for the Educationally Sub-normal that he worked in, he did not recall seeing any pupil of an 'Indian/South Asian' appearance and who might therefore have been of Caribbean Indian descent. What drove BC to write was his own direct personal experience in ESN schools. The focus of the work, therefore, was clearly the plight of 'West Indian' children of African descent, males in particular. In 1967, immigrant children made up 15 per cent of the enrolment in British schools, and about 28.4 per cent of the enrolment in ESN schools. In other words, immigrant children were overrepresented in ESN schools by a ratio of nearly 2 (28.4/15 = 1.89). However, for Black Caribbean children, the overrepresentation in ESN schools was even worse, at 2.63 to 1.

» What Happened When 'West Indian' Turned 'Black Caribbean'

We fast-forward 50 years. The labels of ethnic categories in the official education statistics have changed, and the category most closely aligned with BC's 'West Indian' is now 'Black Caribbean', a subgroup of 'Black'. The statistics cover the mean scores (out of 90) for the GCSE in 8 subjects across ethnic and gender groups within the entire UK for 2019.[23] Compared to the national average scores of 44.0 and 49.5 for 'All' Male and Female pupils, respectively, Black Caribbean pupils are underperforming (35.7 and 43.2 for Males and Females, respectively), with the level of under-performance being greater for Males (8.3 versus 6.3).

23 GOV.UK, 2020.

The gender gap is ever present. Across all the groups, Females perform better than Males. The gap ranges from a low of 3.2 for 'Chinese' to a high of 8.5 for 'Black Other', and the overall average for 'All' is 4.5. Thus, the gender gap of 7.5 for 'Black Caribbean' is large. The general trend is that the lower performing groups have bigger gender gaps – or, to put it another way, the higher the level of performance of the group, the smaller the difference between the genders.

The report of the Programme for International Student Assessment[24] shows what is well known, namely, that, across the 79 countries participating in its test, the higher up the socio-economic scale a pupil is, the better the performance on academic tests. We refer now to the statistics on the 2019 mean scores for the GCSE in 8 subjects across ethnic and gender groups across the entire UK[25] as presented from the GOV.UK (2020) table 'Average Attainment Age score (out of 90) by ethnicity and sex', which includes the variable, 'Eligibility for Free School Meals (FSM)' and provide a breakdown by ethnicity and FSM eligibility. Since free school meals are provided to pupils from economically impoverished backgrounds, eligibility for such meals is a handy measure of socio-economic status. In the data, across all ethnic groups, those eligible for school meals have a lower mean score than those who are not. An interesting detail is that, among those eligible for such meals, the average score for 'White British' is 31.8, whereas that for 'Black Caribbean' is 34.1. Contrary to expectation, in this category, working class Black Caribbean children outperform their working class White British counterparts.

We do not have figures for the above 2019 data on the combined effects of ethnicity, eligibility for free school means *and* gender. We can, however, deduce these from some earlier studies. One Department of Education study[26] presents the

24 PISA, 2018.
25 GOV.UK, 2020.
26 Dept of Education, GOV.UK, 2015, p. 13.

percentages of pupils across the various ethnic groups who attained 5 GCSE subjects at grades A*– C, including English and Mathematics in the 2013/14 academic year. The figures show that Black Caribbean males eligible for free school meals, at 30.8 per cent, outperform their White British counterparts at 23.8 per cent.[27] In the data presentation in Figure 10 of the Kirby et al. study[28] covering the 2014/2015 examination results, Black Caribbean free-school-meal entitled girls outperform their White British equivalents by at least 10 per cent. There is a pattern here, that at the lowest income level, gender for gender, the Black Caribbean ethnic group seems to be outperforming its White British counterpart.

The interpretation of this finding is unclear. One possibility is that free school meals have a bigger positive impact on the performance of Black Caribbean children than on that of White British children. Another is that we might be seeing some of the indirect effect of the BC (1971) book itself. The community supplementary school movement advocated for by BC 50 years ago in his work subsequently became a force to be reckoned with in the Black Caribbean community. This movement may be responsible for the relative improvement in Black Caribbean academic performance amongst the economically most deprived section of the community.

The original charge made by BC in 1971, in the very title of the work, is that '…the West Indian child is made educationally sub-normal in the British school system'. The driving force behind this process, he argued, was racism. The evidence is that both socio-economic class and racism continue to make Black Caribbean pupils 'perform educationally below the norm'. There is a complication, however. Discrimination in a White British society tends to make Black people economically poor. Pupils from economically impoverished backgrounds perform less well in school. This then sentences them to a life of poverty

27 Dept of Education, Dept of Education, 2015, p. 13.
28 Kirby et al., 2016, p. 5.

as adults. BC's original work sought to tackle both of these from the perspective of the Black Caribbean community and what *it* could do the help itself. Were those efforts successful? The answer is probably a very, very muted and guarded, 'Yes', followed by numerous 'buts'.

And as for the gender effects? Yes, Black Caribbean females are doing better than Black Caribbean males. Whilst true for all ethnic groups, the gender gap within Black Caribbean is especially large. There are two possible conclusions from the fact that the highest performing ethnic groups show the smallest gender differences in performance. One is that continued efforts to raise the level of performance within the Black Caribbean group will narrow the gender gap. The other is that a special effort needs to be made to target Black Caribbean boys and the gender-related attitudes getting in the way of their academic performance. Common sense suggests that a mix of these approaches should be adopted going forward.

❭ What is the Origin of Racism?

BC, in his Chapter 7, addresses an important question, 'Why our children get the worst education – the immigrants' role in Britain'. The goal of BC's work was to drive people to immediate action. He limits his answer to the broader 'why' question by focusing on the UK during the time span of the post-Second World War immigration to Britain. In reality, of course, the story of discrimination against Black Caribbean and other non-white immigrants in the education system and beyond, goes back four centuries. This is to the birth of European and then specifically British colonisation of the Caribbean and the Americas. An estimated 11 million Africans were imported into the Americas and the Caribbean to labour on European-controlled plantations and in mines. Britain emerges, by the mid-17th century, as the front runner in the creation of plantation sugar colonies, first in Barbados and then Jamaica, and from there to the rest of the British possessions in the area, including parts of what is now the USA.

Oppressing other people always needs moral justification. In this case, the British and other Europeans had to explain to themselves and others why they had the right to treat other human beings as property, enslaving not just those who were alive at any point but all their children and their children's children into perpetuity. In this manner, race and racism were born. The concept of being 'white' was invented. Those who were so classified belonged to a class of human who could not be property and whose progeny could be presumed to be automatically also protected from being property. Then there was the category 'Black' invented to designate those who were, by biblical injunction, designated to be hewers of wood and drawers of water, labour to be worked, owned and traded as a matter of right by those designated 'white'. Those who were 'white' were superior and by virtue of whiteness deserved their superior position. Those who were 'Black' were inferior and by being defined thus, also deserving of their assigned lot in life.

Some historians contest the extent to which the British sugar plantations of the Caribbean were central to the financing of the industrial revolution in Britain. What is uncontested, however, is the economic significance for Britain of the trans-Atlantic trade in manufactured goods from Europe, enslaved people from West and West Central Africa and plantation goods, notably sugar, produced by African and African-descended enslaved workers in the British Caribbean. This trading system became the base for British trading and colonial expansion into the Indian and Pacific oceans, and the emergence by the 19th century of the British Empire 'on which the sun never sets'. Britannia ruled the waves. Britons would never be slaves but made their wealth as entitled 'white' people through the sweat and labour of 'Black' people undeserving of any other fate than that of being enslaved labouring property.

Britain abolished slavery in its colonies in 1834. The owners of slaves were compensated to the tune of 20 million pounds, 17 billion pounds in today's currency for their over 800,000 enslaved people, mainly in the Caribbean. Over 300 thousand of these were in Jamaica alone. A loan was taken by the British government to fund the compensation. The enslaved received no compensation and were, in fact, required by the Slavery Abolition Act of 1833 to work for between 4-6 years as unpaid 'apprentices', to further compensate their previous owners for loss of property. Once fully free, these formerly enslaved people found themselves in competition in the labour market with indentured servants imported by the British from Asia, in particular British India.

The formerly enslaved came to constitute a labour force which, over the next century and a half, was deployed around the Atlantic area when cheap and readily available labour was required. They dug the Panama Canal and worked on the banana plantations of the United Fruit Company in Central America during the late 19th and early 20th centuries. They migrated to New York in the early 20th century to join the work force of a rapidly industrialising northern USA. And then, in 1948, came the great labour shortage in post-war Britain and the migration of the 'Windrush' generation 'to rebuild Britain'. The ultimate irony is that, as taxpayers, Caribbean immigrants were made to contribute to the repayment of the twenty-million-pound loan taken out by the British government to compensate owners of enslaved people emancipated in 1834. The Windrush generation, through their taxes, were made to pay for the compensation paid out to the enslavers of their ancestors. The loan taken out by the British government was, in fact, only fully paid off in 2015.

This then was the context within which Black Caribbean children were, in the words of BC, being made educationally subnormal by the British education system. They were 'Black' in a system which said that 'white' was good and 'Black' was bad, one which kept wage rates down by paying Black workers less than Whites, even while duping white workers into thinking how special they were to be, by virtue of their skin colour, earning more than Blacks.

In Chapter 8, he provides an action list entitled, 'What we can do for ourselves'. At the top of that list is the setting up of nursery schools as well as supplementary schools functioning on weekends. BC's work was the manifesto of the supplementary school movement which swept the Black Caribbean community in Britain, particularly during the 1980s to '90s. These supplementary schools came to be adopted by other ethnic minority communities of immigrant background with great success. This can be seen from the already presented education statistics for these groups.

That non-white ethnic groups of immigrant background, including Black Caribbean, are doing as well as they are, can be seen as a victory for struggle against racial oppression. The fact of this supposed 'over-performance' has become the subject of official concern as seen in the interestingly-titled 2015 document from the UK Department of Education, 'A compendium of research on ethnic minority resilience to the effects of deprivation on attainment: A Research Report'.[29] As the document states in its overview, 'The lower educational achievement of White working class pupils in comparison with children from other ethnic backgrounds with similar socio-economic status continues to attract attention...'(p. 1). Ironically, 50 years on, it is the White British working class that is the object of greatest official concern in the educational stakes.

Adopting the Figueroa (2012)[30] argument as it applies to gender and performance in Jamaica to ethnicity, a sense of entitlement, whether on the ground of gender or, here, on the ground of race, is an enemy to academic achievement in

29 Stokes et al., 2015.

30 Mark Figueroa, *Underachieving Caribbean Boys: Marginalisation or gender privileging?* (2012), pp. 23-25.

a system which is moving towards equality of opportunity. The 'resilience' in the Department of Education[31] documents includes what they refer to as 'social capital'. With reference to Chinese, the top performing ethnic group, this social capital is identified as involving attendance at supplementary schools in addition to close family and community networks. Also identified as aiding the minorities of immigrant background is their willingness to pay for private tutoring. Many of these community behaviours, described as cases of 'resilience', did not all occur naturally. Some, notably supplementary schools, were the result of the kind of advocacy found in the 1971 work by BC and deliberate action on the part of community activists. They have been developed and fostered by non-white ethnic immigrant communities to defy the downward gravitational pull of societal racism on the educational opportunities of their children. The resilience so lauded in the document[32] is, at least in part, really a product of struggle by the various non-White ethnic groups against racism.

❱ What New Forms of Struggle and To What End?

Britain, up to 75 years ago, ruled the largest empire the world had ever seen. It now has an education system which is in 12th place according to the Programme for International Student Assessment (PISA) 2018 rankings. Countries and/or regions of countries with over 550M of the world's population outperform the UK on reading skills tested in the 2018 PISA test. Ahead in the ranking are several provinces of China, in addition to Hong Kong, Macau and Singapore. The two top European countries in positions higher up than the UK are Estonia and Finland, both countries without a colonial past. I would speculate that, without the burden of an imperial legacy and a colonially induced sense of superiority, these European

31 Stokes et al., 2015.
32 Stokes et al., 2015, p. 24.

countries have been freer to rethink, reform and innovate within their education systems.

Against the background of everything that has been said so far, I would suggest that people of non-White immigrant origin from the former empire now living in the UK, hold the key to a better future for the British education system. This is particularly true of the descendants of enslaved Africans, people of Black Caribbean origin, on the backs of whose ancestors modern Britain was built. Radical reform is necessary to make a UK education system which is non-racist, anti-racist, world class and open to all. Such reform would benefit, most of all, the majority ethnic group, White British, stuck in the self-destructive role granted by White privilege, that of over-compensated underperformers. How to achieve this has to be the subject of another and longer discussion.

— HUBERT DEVONISH

Dept. of Language, Linguistics and Philosophy
The University of the West Indies,
Mona Campus, Jamaica

January 13, 2021

Appendix I: Tables

❱ Table 1

***Immigrant Pupils in Ordinary and ESN Day Schools,
September 1966 and 1967***

Year	School type	No. of pupils on roll	No. of immigrant pupils	Percentage of immigrants
1966	Ordinary	398,133	52,400	13.2
	ESN	3,876	904	23.3
1967	Ordinary	397,130	59,434	15.0
	ESN	4.109	1,166	28.4

❱ Table 2

***Nationality of Immigrant Pupils in Ordinary and
ESN Schools, Spring 1967***

Nationality	Ordinary schools	ESN schools
West Indian	54%	75%
Indian and Pakistani	10%	4%
Cypriot	16%	13%
Other	21%	8%
Total no. of children	55,161	886

Appendix II:
BOOK LIST FOR PARENTS
West Indian Literature for Children

Books and book lists with prices are obtainable from:

New Beacon Books Ltd.
76 Stroud Green Road,
Finsbury Park, London N4 3EN
Tel. 207-272-4889
Email: newbeaconbooksuk@gmail.com

❱ NOVELS

❱ *Hurricane*

❱ *Drought*

❱ *Fire*

❱ *Riot*

Four adventure novels for children by Andrew Salkey, about the experiences of children from different families during the exciting events of hurricane, fire, drought, and a riot in a marketplace. Set in town and country in Jamaica. Suitable for 8- to 12-year-olds. *Hurricane* received the German Children's Book Prize in 1968.

❱ *The Year in San Fernando* by Michael Anthony

Excellent novel about the experiences, of a 12-year-old boy who leaves his home in the country for San Fernando, a large town in Trinidad. Suitable for 12- to 16-year-olds.

❱ *Black Midas* by Jan Carew, a Guyanese author

> *Anansi Stories* and *West Indian Folk Tales*, both by Philip Sherlock

> *West Indian Stories* by Andrew Salkey

> *Caribbean Narrative* by O. R. Dathorne

> *West Indian Narrative* by Kenneth Ramchand

These last three (above) are selections of Caribbean writing suitable for secondary school pupils.

> *The Sun's Eye*. Edited by Anne Walmsley

A selection of stories and poetry suitable for 11- to 15-year-olds.

HISTORICAL NOVELS

> *Queen of the Mountain* by P. M. Cousins

An adventure story about the Jamaican Maroons. Very well written. Suitable for 8- to 13-year olds.

> *Sixty-Five* by V. S. Reid

About the excitement of the 1865 rebellion in Jamaica, as seen by a 12-year-old boy.

HISTORY

> *The People Who Came. Book 1* by Alma Norman; and *Book 2* by Patricia Patterson and James Carnegie

A good description of the cultures of India, Africa, China, American Indian tribes, and Europe, and the ways in which they affected the West Indies. For secondary pupils 11 to 14 years old.

> *Marcus Garvey 1887-1940* by Adolph Edwards

The story of the life of the man who preached Black Pride in Jamaica and America and opened our eyes.

> *A Visual History of the West Indies* by Shirley Duncker

Excellent for primary classes.

▶ PLAYS

> *Four Plays for Primary Schools* by Edward Brathwaite

> *Odale's Choice* by Edward Brathwaite

Appendix III:
Resource Organisations

❱ Caribbean Education and Community Workers' Association

West Indian children are being put in disproportionate numbers in the lowest streams of secondary schools; they have been placed in their thousands in ESN schools where the authorities themselves now admit they do not belong; in some boroughs they are being bussed from their neighbourhood to far distant schools; the children have been banded – or bandied – about the school in various boroughs, on the assumption that they are of low intelligence 'and' culturally deprived', and so must be spread in twos and threes throughout the school system to prevent 'standards being lowered'.

All these actions, and many more that we find out about every day, have been done and *continue to be done* without consulting the children's parents. And in many of those cases where parents have to be consulted by law, they have been deceived – for example, the authorities have described the ESN school as 'special', rather than a school for the *subnormal.*

The *Caribbean Education and Community Workers' Association* (CECWA) consists of West Indian teachers, social workers, educational psychologists and community workers. It has three main functions:

> ❯ To do/carry out research and find out what is happening to our children in the schools – and why;

❯ To let all Black parents know what is happening and what their rights are;

❯ To help set up parents and youth organisations all over the country to meet the needs of the Black child – supplementary Black schools, youth clubs, nursery schools, playgroups and so on.

❯ The George Padmore Institute

Although CECWA no longer exists, the George Padmore Institute, part of the same collective of organisations, very much does and is a very useful resource for parents, teachers and the Black community (everyone else as well). If you can help in *any* way, please contact:

George Padmore Institute
76 Stroud Green Road
Finsbury Park, London
N4 3EN

Phone: 020-7272-8915
Email: info@georgepadmoreinstitute.org
Website: www.georgepadmoreinstitute.org

❯ Caribbean Labour Solidarity (CLS)

'We will support all who recognise that the struggle against racism, fascism, imperialism and neo-colonialism in the Caribbean requires the building of strong international links between the working people there and their sisters and brothers globally. In so doing we recognise that the British Empire has bestowed a bitter legacy on sections of the working classes in the UK and the former colonies. We seek to maintain and expand solidarity with the black workers and their allies in the Caribbean as well as being part of the anti-racist struggle in Britain.'

Caribbean Labour Solidarity (CLS)
29 Myddelton Street,
Islington, London
EC1R 1UA

Email: info@cls-uk.org.uk
Website: www.cls-uk.org.uk

❱ Grenada-Forward Ever

'Grenada-Forward Ever will provide assistance to organisations and individuals in Grenada and elsewhere, seeking to advance the material, economic, social and general well-being of the people of Grenada. We invite you to join us...'

Grenada-Forward Ever
c/o 71 Wiltshire Road,
Thornton Heath,
Croydon, Surrey
CR7 7QP

Mobile: 07544-026-122
Email: info@grenada-forwardever.net
Website: www.grenada-forwardever.net

Appendix IV:
Some Supplementary Schools[33]

EAST LONDON

1. **African Community School**
   24-30 Dalston Lane, Dalston, London E8 3AZ

   Phone: 02079 238 350 or 07484 356 541
   Email: office@acschool.org.uk
   Website: www.acschool.org.uk

2. **Alkebu-lan Academy of Excellence**
   282 High Road, Leyton, London, E10 5PW

   Phone: 07908 814 152
   Email: alkebulan.academy@yahoo.co.uk or
                info@alkebulan.org
   Website:
   www.alkebulan.org/alkebu-lan-academy-of-excellence

3. **Eastside Young Leaders' Academy**
   Bignold Hall, Bignold Road, London E7 0EX

   Phone: 020 8522 1000
   Email: info@eyla.org.uk
   Website: www.eyla.org.uk

4. **Garvey Lumumba Academy Online**
   156 Campden Crescent, Becontree, Dagenham, RM8 2SL

   Phone: 07984 342740

---

33 All records are correct as far as could be ascertained at the time of going to print. Compiled by Jacqueline McKenzie using several data sources including those of the National Association of Black Supplementary Schools and the National Resource Centre for Supplementary Education, with assistance from Akhita Benjamin, senior training consultant and expert on supplementary schools, and Tumaini Joseph.

NORTH LONDON

5. **African Community School**
   Princess May Primary School
   Stoke Newington, Hackney, London N16 8DF

   Phone: 07484 356 541 or 02079 238 350
   Email: office@acschool.org.uk
   Website: www.acschool.org.uk

6. **Lemuel Findlay Supplementary School**
   The College of Haringey, Enfield & North East London
   (CONEL), Tottenham Centre, High Road
   London N15 4RU

   Phone: 07944 204 876
   Email: admin@lfss.org.uk
   Website: www.lfss.org.uk

7. **Mandela Supplementary School**
   27-30 Cheriton, Queen's Crescent, London NW5 4EZ

   Phone: 020 7284 0030
   Email: mandela@thecarafcentre.co.uk,
   admin@thecarafcentre.org.uk
   Website: www.thecarafcentre.co.uk

SOUTH LONDON

8. **Afruika Bantu Saturday School (ABSS)**[34]
   St Martins Community Centre,
   Abbots Park, Upper Tulse Hill, SW2 3PW

   Phone: 07903 012 757
   Email: kayode.abss@gmail.com
   Website: afruikabantusaturdayschool.weebly.com

---

34 Tumaini Joseph's parents were among the many who founded
   Supplementary Schools, and Tumaini, who is the science teacher at
   ABSS, was himself a student of that school as a child.

9. **Nubian African Community Saturday School**
   Springfield Community School,
   110 Union Road, London SW8 2SH

   Phone: 07931 238 759 or 07894 555 186
   Email: info@nubiasaturdayschool.com
   Website: www.nubiasaturdayschool.org

10. **The Learning Cube**
    The Woodlawns Centre,
    16 Leigham Court Road, London SW16 6PJ

    Phone: 07505 489 568 or 07961 148 568
    Email: admin@thelearningcube.org.uk
    Website: www.thelearningcube.org.uk
               www.facebook.com/thelearningcube/

11. **Karibu Education Centre**
    7 Gresham Road, London SW9 7PH

    Phone: 020 7733 9423
    Email: karibucentre@gmail.com
    Website: www.karibueducationcentre.org.uk

12. **Manna Supplementary School**
    Bethel House, Lansdowne Place, London, SE1 4XH

    Phone: 07539 827515 or 020 3417 3324
    Email: mannaborn2shine@gmail.com
    Website: www.facebook.com/mannaborn2shine

13. **Southside Young Leaders' Academy**
    Walworth Academy, Shorncliffe Road, London SE1 5UJ

    Phone: 020 7701 9055
    Email: info@syla.org.uk
    Website: www.syla.org.uk

14. **The Youth Learning Network**
    Goose Green Community Centre
    62A East Dulwich Road, London SE22 9AT

    Phone: 07821 623 009
    Email: info@youthlearningnetwork.org
    Website: www.youthlearningnetwork.org

WEST LONDON

15. **Descendants Supplementary School**
    Acton Gardens Community Centre, Unit A, Munster
    Court, Office Room 3, Bollo Bridge Road, W3 8UU

    Phone: 07745 889521 or 07818 251138
    Email: descendants93@gmail.com
    Website: www.descendants.org.uk

16. **Westside Young Leaders Academy**
    [Saturday school only] Capital City Academy, Doyle
    Gardens, Willesden, London, NW10 3ST
    [Postal address only] Westside Young Leaders Academy
    c/o Tall Horse Accounts Ltd, SBC House, Restmor Way,
    Wallington SM6 7AH

    Phone: 07508 528 054
    Email: contact@wylauk.com, wylacademy@gmail.com
    Website: www.wylauk.com

17. **Willesden Supplementary Saturday School**
    165–167 High Road, Willesden, London, NW10 2SD

    Phone: 07956 649 360 or 07961 560 581
    Email: ianlewinson@hotmail.co.uk, eyemissy@aol.co.uk
    Website: www.wntcg.org/school

BIRMINGHAM

18. **Children of the Sun Supplementary School**
    339 Dudley Road, Birmingham, B18 4HB

    Phone: 07933 823 505
    Email: marcia.anderson21@yahoo.com
             childrenofthesunsaturdayschool@gmail.com
    Website:
          www.facebook.com/childrenofthesunsaturdayschool

BUCKINGHAMSHIRE

19. Akacia Complementary School
    Hilltop Community Centre, Crest Road,
    High Wycombe, Bucks, HP11 1UA

    Phone: 0794 6966600 or 07970 050490
    Email: denkar.stew@hotmail.co.uk
    Website: www.hilltophighwycombe.org/akacia-school

LEICESTER

20. Phoenix Agenda Supplementary School
    African Caribbean Cultural Centre
    Maidstone Road, Leicester LE2 0UA

    Phone: 07552 917030
    Email: kaiteura@gmail.com,
             phoenixagendasupplementaryschool@hotmail.com
    Website: www.phoenixagendaschool.com

MANCHESTER

21. Highway Hope Supplementary School
    1 Matthews Lane, Levenshulme, Manchester M12 4QW

    Phone: 07723 447200 or 0161 248 7733
    Email: admin@highwayhope.co.uk
    Website: www.highwayhope.co.uk

22. MEaP Academy Virtual Twilight School
    Brow House, 1 Mabfield Road, Manchester, M14 6LP

    Phone: 0161 759 9918 or 0161 666 0572
    Email: info@meap.org.uk
    Website: www.meap.org.uk

SCOTLAND

23. Kwame Nkrumah Heritage Academy
    3/1, 33 Aberfoyle Street, Glasgow G31 3RW

    Phone: 07552 917 030
    Email: elmensah@yahoo.com
    Website: www.facebook.com/nkrumahacademy

ONLINE

24. **Accoutre Centre for Learning**

    Phone: 07572 859 639
    Email: info@accoutre.org.uk
    Website: www.accoutre.org.uk

25. **Black Teachers Tutor**

    Website: www.blackteacherstutor.co.uk

26. **Moore Education**

    Email: contact@mooreeducation.co.uk
    Website: www.mooreeducation.co.uk
               www.facebook.com/mooreeducation01

27. **Rise Education**

    Phone: 07399 526 072
    Email: info@rise-tuition.co.uk
    Website: www.rise-tuition.co.uk

28. **Simon Education**

    Phone: 07944 504 501
    Website: www.simoneducation.com
               www.facebook.com/SimonEducationHQ

❱ National Association of Black Supplementary Schools (NABSS)

NABSS provides a directory of supplementary schools all over the UK. It was set up in 2007 to ensure more parents have the opportunity to enrol their children into these schools so they can get the full, rich African-centred education they deserve.

National Association of Black Supplementary Schools
37 Chapel Street, London NW1 5DP

Phone: 07958-348-558
Email: info@nabss.org.uk
Website: www.nabss.org.uk

Bibliography[35]

Bagley, C., 'The educational performance of immigrant children'. Comment on ILEA Report. *Race, Vol. 10*, No. 1, July 1968, pp. 91-94.

Baratz, S., 'Effect of race of experimenter, instructions, and comparison population upon level of reported anxiety in negro subjects'. *Journal of Personality and Social Psychology, Vol. 7*, No. 2, October 1967, pp. 194-196.

Bergman, C., 'Colonial colleges'. *Times Educational Supplement*, November 6, 1970, p. 53.

Bhatnagar, J., *Immigrants at School*. London: Cornmarket Press, 1970.

Bibby, C. *Race, Prejudice and Education*. Heinemann, 1959.

Biesheuvel, S. & R. Liddicoat, 'The effects of cultural factors on intelligence test performance'. *Journal of the National Institute Personnel Research, Vol. 8*, No. 1, September 1959, pp. 3-14.

Bowker, G. *The Education of Coloured Immigrants*. Longmans, 1968.

Clark, K.B. & M.P. Clark, 'Racial identification and preference in Negro children'. In Newcomb, T.M. & Hartley, E.L. (eds), *Readings in Social Psychology*. New York: Holt, 1947, pp. 169-178.

Coffman, W.E., 'Developed tests for the culturally different'. *School and Society, Vol. 93*, November 13, 1965, pp. 430-433.

Daniel, W.W., 'Racial discrimination in England'. Based on a P.E.P. Report. Penguin, 1968.

Davis, A., 'Poor people have brains too'. *The Phi Delta Kappan, Vol. 30*, No. 8, April 1949, pp. 294-95.

Derrick, J., *Teaching English to Immigrant Children*. Longmans, 1966.

Deutsch, M., I. Katz, & A.R. Jensen (eds), *Social Class, Race and Psychological Development*. Holt, Reinhart & Winston 1968.

Dreger, R.M. & K.S. Miller, 'Comparative psychological studies of Negroes and whites in the United States'. *Psychology Bulletin, Vol. 57*, September 1960, pp. 361-402.

---

35 Where possible, the errors of the 2nd edition bibliography have been corrected. Publications mentioned in parts 2 and 3 have been added.

Evans, P.C. & R.B. Le Page, 'The education of West Indian immigrant children'. *National Committee for Commonwealth Education*, 1967.

Ferron, O.M. 'The linguistic factor in the test intelligence of West African children'. *Educational Research, Vol. 9*, No. 2, February 1967, pp. 113-121.

_____. 'The test performance of "coloured" children'. *Educational Research, Vol. 8*, No. 1, November 1965, pp. 42-57.

Figueroa, M. (2012), *Underachieving Caribbean Boys: Marginalisation or gender privileging?* Commonwealth Education Partnership 2007, pp. 23-25. https://www.cedol.org/wp-content/uploads/2012/02/23-25-2007.pdf. Retrieved 13 January, 2021.

Frazer, E., *Home Environment and the School*. London: University of London Press, 1968.

Gillborn, D., 'Education policy as an act of white supremacy: whiteness, critical race theory and education reform'. *Journal of Education Policy, Vol. 20*, No. 4, July 2005.

Gillborn, D. & D. Youdell, *Rationing Education: Policy, Practice, Reform and Equity*. Buckingham: Open University Press, 2000.

Goldman, R.T. & F.M. Taylor, 'Coloured immigrant children: A survey of research, studies and literature on their educational problems and potential in Britain'. *Educational Research, Vol. 8*, No. 3, 1966, pp. 163-183.

Goodman, M.E., *Race Awareness in Young Children*. Cambridge, Massachusetts: Addison-Wesley, 1952. Collier Books, 1964.

Gordon, L.V. & A. Kikuchi, 'American personality tests in cross-cultural research – A caution'. *Journal of Social Psychology, Vol. 69*, No. 2, August 1966, pp. 179-183.

GOV.UK, 'GCSE and equivalent attainment by pupil characteristics, 2013 to 2014' (Revised). 'GCSE and equivalent attainment by pupil characteristics: 2014'. Dept of Education, 2015. https://www.gov.uk/government/statistics/gcse-and-equivalent-attainment-by-pupil-characteristics-2014. Retrieved 13 January 2021.

_____, 'GCSE results ("Attainment 8") – GOV.UK Ethnicity facts and figures'. 2020. https://www.ethnicity-facts-figures.service.gov.uk/education-skills-and-training/11-to-16-years-old/gcse-results-attainment-8-for-children-aged-14-to-16-key-stage-4/latest#title. Retrieved 13 January 2021.

Grinder, R.E., W. Spotts, & M. Curtis, 'Relationships between

Goodenough Draw-a-man Test performance and skin colour among pre-adolescent Jamaican children'. *Journal of Social Psychology,* Vol. 62, 1964, pp. 181-188.

Hicks, R.E., 'Some comments on test developments in emerging countries: With special reference to Papua and New Guinea'. *Papua and New Guinea Journal of Education,* Vol 6, No 3, October 1969, pp. 29-43.

Houghton, V.P. 'Intelligence testing of West Indian and English children'. *Race, Vol. 8,* No. 2, October 1966, pp. 147-156.

Howard, L.R.C. & W.A. Roland, 'Some inter-cultural differences on the Draw-a-man Test: Goodenough scores'. *Man, Vol. 54,* No. 127, June 1964, pp. 86-88.

Hudson, L., 'IQ: The effect of heredity and environment'. *The Times Saturday Review,* November 7, 1970.

Inner London Education Authority, *The Education of Immigrant Pupils in Special Schools for ESN Children.* Report 657. London: ILEA, September 10, 1968.

_____, *The Education of Immigrant Pupils in Primary Schools.* Report 959. London: ILEA, February 12, 1968.

Jahoda, G., T. Veness, & I. Pushkin, 'Awareness of ethnic differences in young children: Proposals for a British study'. *Race, Vol. 8,* No. 1, July 1966, pp. 63-74.

Jones, K. & A.D. Smith, *Economic Impact of Commonwealth Immigration,* National Institute of Economic and Social Research (NIESR) Occasional Paper Vol. 24. Cambridge University Press, 1970.

Kaplan, L. 'Social class influences on mental health'. Section on 'Intelligence and social status'. In *Mental Health and Human Relations in Education,* Chapter 8. New York : Harper & Ross, 1959.

Kirby, Philip et al. (2016), 'Class differences: Ethnicity and disadvantage'. *Research Brief,* No. 14, November 2016, p. 1-6. https://www.suttontrust.com/wp-content/uploads/2016/11/Class-differences-report_References-available-online.pdf Retrieved 13 January 2021.

Klineberg, O. 'Negro-white differences in intelligence test performance: A new look at an old problem.' *American Psychologist, Vol. 18,* No. 4, April 1963, pp. 198-203.

Lesser, G.S., G. Fifer, & D.H. Clark, 'Mental abilities of children from different social-class and cultural groups'. *Monographs of the*

Society for Research in Child Development, Vol. 30, No. 4. University of Chicago Press, 1965.

Little, A., C. Mabey, & G. Whitaker, 'The education of immigrant pupils'. *Race, Vol. 9*, No. 4, October 1968, pp. 439-452.

Loeb, M.B., 'Implications of status differentiation for personal and social development'. *Harvard Educational Review, Vol. 23*, Summer 1953, pp. 168-174.

Maxwell, M., 'Violence in the toilets: Experiences of a Black teacher in Brent schools'. *Race Today, Vol. 1*, January 1969, pp. 135-139.

Munford, W.B. & C.E. Smith, 'Racial comparisons and intelligence testing'. *African Affairs, Vol. 37*, January 1938, pp. 46-57.

National Association of Schoolmasters, *Special Report. Education and the Immigrants*. London, 1969.

National Union of Teachers, Pamphlet: 'The Ascertainment of ESN Children'. 1967.

Oakley, R. (ed.), *New Backgrounds – The Immigrant Children at Home and at School*. Oxford University Press for the Institute of Race Relations, 1968.

Office of National Statistics (2019), Ethnicity Pay Gaps in Great Britain, Ethnicity pay gaps in Great Britain – Office for National Statistics. https://www.ons.gov.uk/employmentandlabourmarket/peopleinwork/earningsandworkinghours/articles/ethnicitypaygapsingreatbritain/2018. Retrieved 13 January 2021.

Peach, C., *West Indian Migration to Britain: A Social Geography*. Oxford University Press, 1968.

Power, J., *Immigrants in School*. Councils and Educational Press, 1967.

Pritchard, D.G., *Education and the Handicapped 1760-1960*. Routledge, 1963.

Programme for International Student Assessment (PISA) (2018), PISA 2018 Results Executive Summary https://www.oecd.org/pisa/Combined_Executive_Summaries_PISA_2018.pdf; https://www.oecd.org/pisa/publications/pisa-2018-results-volume-ii-b5fd1b8f-en.htm. Retrieved 13 January 2021.

Radke, M.J. & H.G. Trager, 'Children's perceptions of the social roles of Negroes and whites'. *Journal of Psychology, Vol. 29*, No. 1, 1950, pp. 3-33.

Rampton, A., *West Indian Children In Our Schools*, HMSO (Cmnd 8273), 1981.

Rosenthal, R. & L.F. Jacobson, 'Teacher expectations for the disadvantaged', *Scientific American, Vol. 218*, No. 4, April 1968, pp.19-23.

Schools Council Working Paper 29, 'Teaching English to West Indian Children'. London: Evans/Metheun Educational, 1970.

Schwarz, P.A., 'Adapting tests to the cultural setting'. *Educational and Psychological Measurement, Vol. 23*, No. 4, 1963, pp. 673-686.

Shuey, A.M., *The Testing of Negro Intelligence* (2nd edn). New York: Social Science Press, 1966.

Stokes, Lucy et al. (2015). A Compendium of Evidence on Ethnic Minority Resilience to the Effects of Deprivation on Resilience: Research Report. Department for Education. https://assets. publishing.service.gov.uk/government/uploads/system/uploads/ attachment_data/file/439861/RR439A-Ethnic_minorities_and_ attainment_the_effects_of_poverty.pdf. Retrieved 12 January 2021.

Stone, M., *West Indian Children in an ESN School Why are they there?* Mimeographed (n.d.).

Tansley, A.E. & R. Gulliford, *The Education of Slow Learning Children.* London: Routledge & Kegan Paul, 1960.

Vaizey, J., 'Social inequality, democracy and education'. *Education in the Modern World.* London: World University Library, 1967, pp. 165-189.

Vernon, P.E., *Selection for Secondary Education in Jamaica: A Report to the Minister of Education.* Kingston: Government Printer 1961.

Watson, P., 'The new IQ test'. *New Society*, Nos. 2&3, January 22, 1970.

_____. 'Race and intelligence'. *New Society*, No. 407, July 16, 1970.

Wein, N., 'Compensatory education'. *Race Today, Vol. 2*, No. 3, March 1970, pp. 72-75.

Wiles, S., 'Children from overseas'. *IRR Newsletter*, February & June 1968.

Williams, P., 'The ascertainment of educationally subnormal children'. *Educational Research, Vol. 7*, No. 2, 1965, pp. 136-146.

About the Author[36]

BERNARD COARD was born in 1944 on the Caribbean island of Grenada. He studied Economics at Brandeis University (USA, 1963-'66) and Comparative Politics and Development Economics at Sussex University (United Kingdom, 1966-'71). While in Britain, Bernard wrote the seminal work, *How the West Indian Child Is Made Educationally Subnormal in the British School System,*[37] helped organise Black Caribbean parents and youth groups, and set up Saturday Supplementary Schools for Black children throughout Britain.

On returning to the Caribbean, Bernard taught at the University of the West Indies (UWI) in Trinidad and Tobago, and at Mona, Jamaica. During that period, Bernard was also actively involved in the formation of the New Jewel Movement (NJM) and was a member of its first (political) bureau. He won the seat of the Town of St. George, Grenada's capital, in the parliament in the December 1976 General Elections, representing the NJM and the 'People's Alliance'.

Bernard played a leading role in the organisation of the NJM for the overthrow of Grenada's dictator, Eric Gairy, on March 13,

---

36 Photo courtesy of Clinton Hutton.

37 First edition by New Beacon Books, 1971. Second edition by Karia Press, London,1991; and republished in 2005 and again in 2007 jointly by Bookmarks Publications and Trentham Books, London, as part of Brian Richardson (Ed.), *Tell It Like It Is: How Our Schools Fail Black Children.*

1979.[38] He was Deputy Prime Minister and Minister of Finance during the Revolution's four years and seven months. He has been widely praised for his handling of the economy during that period, and for the many economic and social programmes that he initiated.

Bernard spent 26 years in prison (1983-2009) following the October 1983 US invasion of Grenada in the aftermath of the tragic killing of Prime Minister and revolutionary leader, Maurice Bishop and several others. The US-orchestrated trial of him and 16 of his colleagues was described by Amnesty International as '...a process that was in gross violation of international standards'.[39]

While in prison, on the initiative of the then Commissioner of Prisons, Mr Winston Courtney, Bernard set up a comprehensive education programme for all inmates, from basic literacy to postgraduate degrees from London University.

Bernard, along with the final group of 'Grenada-17' political prisoners, was finally released on September 5, 2009. Since then, he has lived in Jamaica with Phyl, his wife, where they celebrated 52 years of marriage when she passed away in 2020. They have three children and four grandchildren. He continues to write (he has so far published three volumes of memoirs 2017-2020)[40] and to teach as a guest lecturer on university courses both within Jamaica and as far as Australia (online).

38 See Layne, *We Move Tonight* (2014).

39 See Amnesty International, *The Grenada 17: Last of the Cold War Prisoners?* (London, October, 2003). For information on the US role in the Grenada-17 judicial process in Grenada, see relevant US Declassified Documents through The Committee for Human Rights in Grenada (CHRG), London.

40 See overleaf.

Other Publications by the Author

With Phyllis Coard
GETTING TO KNOW OURSELVES
Bogle L'Ouverture Publications, London, 1971
(Children's Book)

THE GRENADA REVOLUTION:
What Really Happened?
McDermott Publishing, Kingston, 2017
(Available from Amazon.com)

FORWARD EVER: Journey To A New Grenada
McDermott Publishing, Kingston, 2018
(Available from Amazon.com)

SKYRED: A Tale Of Two Revolutions
McDermott Publishing, Kingston, 2020
(Available from Amazon.com)

Forthcoming

FROM UNDERACHIEVERS TO TOP PERFORMERS:
The Story of the Richmond Hill Prison
Education Programme

STORMY WEATHER: My Personal Story

Notes ...

Notes...

Notes ...

Notes...